Making Sin Exceeding Sinful

What Must Our Sin Look Like?

Dr. Gary L. Mann

Formatting and Publishing assisted by
The Old Paths Publications, Inc.
Cleveland, GA 30528
Web address: www.theoldpathspublications.com
Email: TOP@theoldpathspublications.com
Office Phones: 706-865-0153 or 706-219-2153
Cell Phone: 706-461-1611

1.0

DEDICATION

This book is dedicated to my parents, Francis and Eleanor Mann and to my wife's parents Gene and Charylene Skaggs. They all have helped me so much in my life and ministry and have been some of my biggest supporters through the years of serving our Lord. Sherry and I love them very much and thank them for their unending love and encouragement.

O GOD OF GRACE

Thou hast imputed my sin to my Substitute, and hast imputed His righteousness to my soul, clothing me with a bridegroom's robe, decking me with jewels of holiness.

But in my Christian walk I am still in rags; my best prayers are stained with sin; my penitential tears are so much impurity; my confessions of wrong are so many aggravations of sin; my receiving the Spirit is tinctured with selfishness.

I need to repent of my repentance; I need my tears to be washed; I have no robe to bring to cover my sins, no loom to weave my own righteousness;

I am always standing clothed in filthy garments, and by grace am always receiving change of raiment, for thou dost always justify the ungodly;

I am always going into the far country, and always returning home as a prodigal, always saying, Father, forgive me, and thou art always bringing forth the best robe.

Every morning let me wear it, every evening return in it, go out to the day's work in it, be married in it, be wound in death in it, stand before the great white throne in it, enter heaven in it shining as the sun.

Grant me never to lose sight of the exceeding sinfulness of sin, the exceeding righteousness of salvation, the exceeding glory of Christ, the exceeding beauty of holiness, the exceeding wonder of grace.

-Author unknown-

"If our righteousness looks like filthy rags to God –

I wonder what our sins look like?"

Dr. G.L. Mann

TABLE OF CONTENTS

INTRODUCTION

As I lay in bed early in the morning thinking about how God must see us, the thought came to me that if our righteousness looks like filthy rags to God, I wonder what our sins look like? Needless to say, I did not get much rest that night. After thinking about this for a while, I thought of the verse in Romans 7:13 which says,

> *"Was then that which is good made death unto me? God forbid. But sin, that it might appear sin, working death in me by that which is good; that sin by the commandment might become exceeding sinful."*

I believe we have entered into a generation where sin is acceptable and really not so bad...and I am not only talking about the lost person's attitude, but the saved person's attitude as well. Indeed some of the reasons for this downward spiral has to do with our society where, as found in Isaiah 5:20, it warns,

> *"Woe unto them that call evil good, and good evil; that put darkness for light, and light for darkness; that put bitter for sweet, and sweet for bitter!"*

I fear our world has degenerated as found in Romans 1:32 from the rejection of God, which is also the basic premise of secular humanism, to,

> *"Who knowing the judgment of God, that they which commit such things are worthy of death, not only do the same, but have pleasure in them that do them."*

With all the influence of the movie industry, television, music and the internet, literally everything goes and immorality is now moral, murder and death are no longer shocking and sin has just become a natural part of everyday life where anything goes. But even more devastating than that, is that we have a view of sin in Christendom that is accepting and agreeable with the worlds concept of sin as not being so sinful. After all, this is a new century and we must not be so out of date.

I must re-ask the question, if our righteousness looks like filthy rags to God, then what must our sins look like? I must also ask the question, where is the thunder from the preachers warning people about sin? With the watered down version of sin that is prevalent today from our preachers, combined with the humanistic views being more acceptable so as to be viewed as politically correct, sin is not exceeding sinful anymore.

Thus, I have endeavored to put some of the sting back into sin with the chapters of this book. May we get back to not only making sin exceeding sinful in our preaching, but may it also become exceeding sinful in our daily walk. This dark world must have light and as the moon reflects the light to the earth from the sun, may we as Christians reflect the light from the Son to the dark world we live in by our walk in holy living once again.

CHAPTER ONE

The Relationship Between the Law and Sin

Romans 7:7-13

What shall we say then? Is the law sin? God forbid. Nay, I had not known sin, but by the law: for I had not known lust, except the law had said, Thou shalt not covet. But sin, taking occasion by the commandment, wrought in me all manner of concupiscence. For without the law sin was dead. For I was alive without the law once: but when the commandment came, sin revived, and I died. And the commandment, which was ordained to life, I found to be unto death. For sin, taking occasion by the commandment, deceived me, and by it slew me. Wherefore the law is holy, and the commandment holy, and just, and good. Was then that which is good made death unto me? God forbid. But sin, that it might appear sin, working death in me by that which is good; that sin by the commandment might become exceeding sinful.

Most people do not truly understand the relationship between the law of God and sin. Because of a false teaching on how to go to heaven, most people believe that if they do their best to keep the Ten Commandments then they will go to heaven. They believe that the law of God is the formula for getting to heaven when the Scriptures clearly teach in Galatians 2:21,

"I do not frustrate the grace of God: for if righteousness come by the law, then Christ is dead in vain."

It is clear here, and in other places, that the law, and the keeping of the law DOES NOT get anyone to heaven. This is not the purpose of the law. Look at the following verses with this in mind.

Galatians 2:16

Knowing that a man is not justified by the works of the law, but by the faith of Jesus Christ, even we have believed in Jesus Christ, that we might be justified by the faith of Christ, and not by the works of the law: for by the works of the law shall no flesh be justified

Ephesians 2:8 & 9

For by grace are ye saved through faith; and that not of yourselves: it is the gift of God:

Not of works, lest any man should boast.

Christ died on the cross to pay for our sins. If we could get saved and go to heaven by always trying to obey the law, which always brings great frustration in a person's life which will be explained later, then, according to Galatians 2:21, "Christ is dead in vain." He did not need to die on the cross IF we could obtain righteousness by the keeping of the law.

I said above that when a person is always trying (which is the key word) to keep the law, it always brings frustration. Why? The answer is quite simple, *we can't!* There is nothing more frustrating than trying to be perfect because, *we can't!* Try as hard as you can to just keep the Ten Commandments and you will always be frustrated because no one can do it – NO ONE!

In James 2:8-11 it states,

"If ye fulfil the royal law according to the scripture, Thou shalt love thy neighbour as thyself, ye do well: But if ye have respect to persons, ye commit sin, and are convinced of the law as transgressors. For whosoever shall keep the whole law, and yet offend in one point, he is guilty of all. For he that said, Do not commit adultery, said also, Do not kill. Now if thou commit no adultery, yet if thou kill, thou art become a transgressor of the law."

There are some very interesting things said in those verses which will be referred to later, but what is important for now is what is found in verse 10 which says, "For whosoever shall keep the whole law, and yet offend in one *point,* he is guilty of all." Any honest person would look at the Ten Commandments and have to admit that, yes, he has broken one or more of the Ten Commandments. Then in agreement of the verse mentioned, if we have broken one of these commands, we are just as guilty as if we had broken them all.

For example, have you ever, at least one time in your life, used the Name of the Lord God in vain? Come on now, be honest! Ok, how about this one. Have you ever lusted after some other persons spouse or looked at someone and lusted? Have you ever one time dishonored your parents? We all have. Then breaking one of these laws ONE TIME makes us a sinner! You might be good in one point of the law but not so good in another. Then you are a sinner! Remember what is says in James 2: 8 & 9?

> *"If ye fulfil the royal law according to the scripture, Thou shalt love thy neighbour as thyself, ye do well: But if ye have respect to persons, ye commit sin, and are convinced of the law as transgressors."*

You are convinced of the law as transgressors! By your actions or thoughts, the law says that you are a sinner! Galatians 3:10 puts it this way…

> *"For as many as are of the works of the law are under the curse: for it is written, Cursed is every one that continueth not in all things which are written in the book of the law to do them."*

Now we are starting to get a true understanding of what the law does in relationship to sin. Now that we are here, let's look again at Romans 7:7-13.

> *"What shall we say then? Is the law sin? God forbid. Nay, I had not known sin, but by the law:*

for I had not known lust, except the law had said, Thou shalt not covet. But sin, taking occasion by the commandment, wrought in me all manner of concupiscence. For without the law sin was dead. For I was alive without the law once: but when the commandment came, sin revived, and I died. And the commandment, which was ordained to life, I found to be unto death. For sin, taking occasion by the commandment, deceived me, and by it slew me. Wherefore the law is holy, and the commandment holy, and just, and good. Was then that which is good made death unto me? God forbid. But sin, that it might appear sin, working death in me by that which is good; that sin by the commandment might become exceeding sinful."

We understand now because of this set of verses that we know what sin is because of the law. Are there other verses that show us this relationship? Let's look at these…

Romans 3:20

" Therefore by the deeds of the law there shall no flesh be justified in his sight: for by the law is the knowledge of sin."

Galatians 3:24

"Wherefore the law was our schoolmaster to bring us unto Christ, that we might be justified by faith. "

The law was not given to tell us what to do, or, how to live to get to heaven. The law was given to show us, or teach us, that we are sinners who sin. Remember, the breaking of the law convinces or convicts us a transgressor. The law is our schoolmaster showing us we are sinners and need a Saviour. Again in verse 7 of Romans 7, "…I had not known sin, but by the law; for I had not known lust except the law had said, Thou shalt not covet." That verse also asks the question "Is the law sin?" The partial answer is, "God forbid." The rest of the answer is found in verses 8 through 11. Then in verse 12 it says,

"Wherefore the law (which is not sin) is holy, and the commandment holy, and just and good." Why? For the very same reason all laws are written, to keep us from harm. In 1 John 5:3 it says,

> *"For this is the love of God, that we keep his commandments: and his commandments are not grievous."*

The commandment, or the law, is not grievous but it is a good thing. Why? Because it teaches us our need of the Saviour since we have transgressed the law – we are sinners. The law warns us of what will ultimately hurt us.

All the signs on the roads we drive are there for our good and for our protection. If I did not have a speed limit sign, I would not know what speed I could drive legally and safely. And, conversely, if I go faster than the limit posted, I am breaking the law and when caught I am responsible for my actions. It is not the law that is sinful or bad, it is the breaking of the law that is bad. In the case of the law of God, it is there to warn me and show me the things that please and displease God. The law is not sin, the breaking of the law is sin, and, as we will see later, sin when it is finished brings death! The law warns me of the things I do and do not do that are sinful and shows me my need of a Saviour!

Before the law was given the law was dead, but again Romans 7:9b says,

> *"...when the commandment came, sin revived, and I died."*

Also in verse 13 is the important statement, "...but sin that it might appear sin..." Paul also wrote, "...for I had not known lust, except the law had said, Thou shalt not covet." Without the law being given to us, we would really not know all that God hates as sin. So the law was given that sin might appear to be sin!

NOW we know what God says is sin and He gave the law to us so we could know what sin is and that we need a Saviour because we are transgressors of the law and are sinners. But that is not all that God wants us to know. He also wanted us to know how foul sin is to Him and how foul it should be to us. Again, in verse 13 it says,

"Was then that which is good made death unto me? God forbid. But sin, that it might appear sin, working death in me by that which is good; that sin by the commandment might become exceeding sinful."

As I have already said a couple of times, and will repeat often in this book, If our righteousness looks like filthy rags to God, what must our sins look like? God gave the law so we would understand what is sinful and that sin is exceeding sinful. It does not matter what sin it is, it is vile to God. He is Holy and wants us to reflect Him as His children by faith in Jesus Christ. We have a tendency to view sin as not so bad but God's view is that sin is exceeding sinful and He wants us to have the same view of sin.

How much does He hate it? In Hebrews 1:9 it says about Jesus,

"Thou hast loved righteousness, and hated iniquity; therefore God, even thy God, hath anointed thee with the oil of gladness above thy fellows."

To the degree that Christ loves righteousness, I would say that at the opposite end of the spectrum that is the degree that He hates sin. He hates sin enough in our lives that He came to the earth to die for our sins, which is a huge amount of love and an awful lot of hate for sin.

William Burkett in his expository notes on the Bible wrote the following on Romans 7:13,

"From what the apostle had said in the former verse, he moves an objection unto this verse: "Seeing the law was holy, and just, and good, how comes it to be unto death?

Was that which was good made death unto me?" To this he replies, both by way of negation, God forbid; for to find fault with the law, is to find fault with God himself! And also by way of affirmation, asserting, that sin is the true cause of death.

The commandment indeed condemns, or is death to the sinner, yet not of itself, but because of sin; as we say of a condemned malefactor, it is not the judge, but the law, that condemns him; or, strictly speaking, it is not the law, but his own guilt, that condemns him; the judge is but the mouth of the law, to denounce the sentence that guilt deserves. And hereby sin appears to be what really it is, sin sinful, exceedingly sinful, masculinely and vigorously sinful, excessively and out of measure sinful, extremely and beyond all expression, nay, beyond our comprehension, sinful.

Learn hence, 1. That the law of God, in the whole, and in every part thereof, is holy in its institution with respect to man: for it was ordained unto life, Ro 7:10.

Learn, 2. That this good and holy law violated and transgressed, condemns and kills, and assigns a person over unto death.

Learn, 3. That though the law condemns man's sin, and man for his sin, yet still the law is good, and not to be blamed; the law is to be justified by man, even when it condemns man: as man had no reason to break the law, so he has no cause to find fault with the law, though it binds him over to death for the breaking of it.

Learn, 4. That 'tis not the law, but sin, that worketh man's death and ruin. Sin aims at not less, and will end in no less; for the wages of sin is death.

Yet, 5. Sin certainly worketh man's death and destruction by that which is good, to wit, the law; for when sin hath used man to break the law, it then makes use of the law to break man; that is, to undo him by condemnation and death for breaking of it.

Lastly, from hence it follows, that sin is therefore exceedingly, yea, unmeasurably sinful, poisonous and pernicious, because it kills men, and not only so, but it kills men by that which is good, to wit, the law. That which was appointed for life, becomes the occasion of death; consequently was in the world.

"Ah! sinful sin, hyperbolically and out of measure sinful, thou art a contempt of God's sovereign authority, a contrariety to his infinite holiness, a violation of his royal and righteous law, and the highest affront that can be offered to the majesty of the great and glorious God.

Thou hast made man like a beast, like the worst of beasts; worse than the worst of beasts; yea, sin is worse than the devil himself, than hell itself. Sin made the devil what he is: A devil and hell never had an existence till sin had one: God was never angry till sin made him angry.

Oh sin! 'tis thou that makest hell to be hell; and the more sin the more hell. Well might the apostle then say here, Sin, that it might appear sin, worketh death in me, and is become exceeding sinful."

John Gill, one of the pastors previous to Charles H. Spurgeon pastoring the Metropolitan Tabernacle wrote,

"Was then that which is good, made death unto me?.... An objection is started upon the last epithet in commendation of the law; and it is as if the objector should say, if the law is good, as you say, how comes it to pass that it is made death, or is the cause of death to you? can that be good, which is deadly, or the cause of death? or can that be the cause of death which is good? This objection taken out of the mouth of another person proceeds upon a mistake of the apostle's meaning; for though he had said that he died when the commandment came, and found by experience that it was unto death, yet does not give the least intimation that the law was the cause of his death; at most, that it was only an occasion, and that was not given by the law, but taken by sin, which, and not the law, deceived him and slew him. Nor is it any objection to the goodness of the law, that it is a ministration of condemnation and death to sinners; for "lex non damnans, non est lex", a law without a sanction or penalty, which has no power to condemn and punish, is no law, or at least a law of no use and service; nor is the judge, or the sentence which he according to law pronounces upon a malefactor, the cause of his death, but the crime which he is guilty of; and the case is the same here, wherefore the apostle answers to this objection with abhorrence and detestation of fixing any such charge upon the law, as being the cause of death to him, saying,

God forbid; a way of speaking used by him, as has been observed, when anything is greatly disliked by him, and is far from his thoughts. Moreover, he goes on to open the true end and reason of sin, by the law working death in his conscience;

but sin, that it might appear sin, working death in me by that which is good; that is, the vitiosity and corruption of nature, which is designed by sin, took an occasion, "by that which is good", that is, the law, through its prohibition of lust, to work in me all manner of concupiscence, which brought forth fruit unto death; wherefore, upon the law's entrance into my heart and conscience, I received the sentence of death in myself, that so sin by it, "working death in me, might appear sin" to me, which I never knew before. This end was to be, and is answered by it, yea,

that sin by the commandment might become exceeding sinful; that the corruption of nature might not only be seen and known to be sin, but exceeding sinful; as being not only contrary to the pure and holy nature of God, but as taking occasion by the pure and holy law of God to exert itself the more, and so appear to be as the words καθ υπερβολην αμαρτωλος, may be rendered, "exceedingly a sinner", or "an exceeding great sinner"; that being the source and parent of all actual sins and transgressions; wherefore not the law, but sin, was the cause of death, which by the law is discovered to be so very sinful."

I will end with these verses from 1 John 3:1-3,

"Behold, what manner of love the Father hath bestowed upon us, that we should be called the sons of God: therefore the world knoweth us not, because it knew him not. Beloved, now are we the sons of God, and it doth not yet appear what we shall be: but we know that, when he shall appear, we shall be like him for we shall see him as he is. <u>And every man that hath this hope in him purifieth himself, even as he is pure."</u>

CHAPTER TWO

O Wretched Man That I Am

Charles H. Spurgeon said:

> "Before I thought upon my soul's salvation, I dreamed that my sins were very few. All my sins were dead, as I imagined, and buried in the graveyard of forgetfulness. But that trumpet of conviction, which aroused my soul to think of eternal things, sounded a resurrection-note to all my sins; and, oh, how they rose up in multitudes more countless than the lands of the sea! Now, I saw that my very thoughts were enough to damn me, that my words would sink me lower than the lowest hell, and as for my acts of sin, they now began to be a stench in my nostrils so that I could not bear them. I thought I had rather have been a frog or a toad than have been made a man. I reckoned that the most defiled creature, the most loathsome and contemptible, was a better thing than myself, for I had so grossly and grievously sinned against Almighty God."

In all the books I have read about the great men of the past there is one common thread, they all felt their sinfulness to a degree that most of us have never even thought of. There was even a loathing of themselves because of their sins in the sight of God, they felt the words, O Wretched Man that I am!

After Paul's teaching on the relationship between the law and sin (Chapter One), we then see him plunge into how sinful he felt he was. Please read all the following verses from Romans 7.

Romans 7:14-24

"For we know that the law is spiritual: but I am carnal, sold under sin.

For that which I do I allow not: for what I would, that do I not; but what I hate, that do I.

If then I do that which I would not, I consent unto the law that it is good.

Now then it is no more I that do it, but sin that dwelleth in me.

For I know that in me (that is, in my flesh,) dwelleth no good thing: for to will is present with me; but how to perform that which

is good I find not.

For the good that I would I do not: but the evil which I would not that I do.

Now if I do that I would not, it is no more I that do it,

but sin that dwelleth in me.

I find then a law, that, when I would do good, evil is present with me.

For I delight in the law of God after the inward man:

But I see another law in my members, warring against the law of my mind, and bringing me into captivity to the law of sin which is in my members.

O wretched man that I am! who shall deliver me from the body of this death?"

Have you ever felt that way? Have you ever felt that it seems like no matter how hard you try, you still sin? I know I have and it can be very disappointing. One of the things I see in 1 John is that when we do not obey the commands it causes us to doubt our salvation. I have often said that there are two reasons why we do not know that we are saved. The first is that we are not saved and the second reason has to do with the fact that we are disobedient in our Christian walk. (That is just a nice way to say that we have sinned.) 1 John 2:3 says,

"And hereby we do know that we know him, if we keep his commandments."

I pointed this out in chapter one but in James 2:9 it states,

"But if ye have respect to persons, ye commit sin, and are convinced of the law as transgressors."

The Greek word for the word "convinced" is also translated in John 8:9 as, "convicted." When we break the law and stand before a judge and jury we are convicted by the law we have broken. In James 2:9 above, we are convinced (convicted) by the law, "as a transgressor." In James 2:11 it states,

"For he that said, Do not commit adultery, said also, Do not kill. Now if thou commit no adultery, yet if thou kill, thou art become a transgressor of the law."

We are not just convinced, we are convicted, and we are guilty and are transgressors of the law!

Taking it a step further, in 1 John 3:4 we read,

"Whosoever committeth sin transgresseth also the law: for sin is the transgression of the law."

Sin is the transgression, or the breaking, of the law. The person who transgresses is the transgressor, the violator, the guilty one! He is convicted!

From the Webster's 1828 dictionary from e-sword on my computer is this definition for transgressor,

"One who breaks a law or violates a command; one who violates any known rule or principle of rectitude; a sinner."

We have transgressed the law. We have broken the law and in doing so are SINNING making us a sinner! Now comes the hard part!

Paul was a saved man when, under the inspiration of God he wrote, "O Wretched Man that I am!" We must not only see sin for what it is in the lost person, but in ourselves also! Sin is exceeding sinful and we must see ourselves as a wretch, EVEN AFTER SALVATION! As I have stated many times before,

Jesus death on the cross delivers us from the penalty of sin but not from the presence of sin! WE STILL SIN! WE ARE STILL TRANSGRESSING THE LAW!

Should we? I mean, now that I am saved and have the gift of eternal life through faith in the substitutionary work of Christ, should I continue in sin? Is it acceptable since I am just a sinner saved by grace? Romans 6:1 & 2 answers that question.

> *"What shall we say then? Shall we continue in sin, that grace may abound?*
>
> *God forbid. How shall we, that are dead to sin, live any longer therein?"*

In the continuing thought about us and our relationship with the law the question is asked in Romans 6:15,

> *"What then? shall we sin, because we are not under the law, but under grace? God forbid"*

More will be said about that later. Even though a person is saved and promised heaven, we must still be on constant guard against sin in our lives. A familiar verse found in Romans 12:1 & 2 clearly states,

> *"I beseech you therefore, brethren, by the mercies of God, that ye present your bodies a living sacrifice, holy, acceptable unto God, which is your reasonable service.*
>
> *And be not conformed to this world: but be ye transformed by the renewing of your mind, that ye may prove what is that good, and acceptable, and perfect, will of God."*

We must be vigilant always recognizing the sinfulness that is still in us and we must yield to our Father at all times and bathe ourselves in prayer and in the Father's love for us and renew our minds so that we can prove what is that good and acceptable and perfect will of God.

Right here I want to point out a false teaching that is prevalent in our ranks about the last part of verse 2 as quoted above. There are some who make the phrase, "…what is that good, and acceptable, and perfect will of God" to mean that there are three levels of the will of God and that if you mess up in one then you can still work on another level. That is not what it teaches! These are not three levels of God's will; they are three descriptions of God's will. Gods will is good, it is acceptable and it is perfect. Teaching like I mentioned gives some the idea that because they failed in one area then they are a second class or even third class Christian who can never do the perfect will of God because they are now below that level. This is just not what the verse teaches. Thank God! I would imagine that if that were so then we would all be below the lowest level of God's will and never able to do His perfect will because of our sinfulness. I am so thankful that He is a longsuffering and merciful Father Who does not accept sin in our lives but remembers we are dust. (Psalm 103:14)

We need to see ourselves as God does and even though a person is saved and promised heaven, we must still guard against sin in our lives. We have weights and the besetting sin which does so easily beset us as found in Hebrews 12:1. We are still in sinful flesh and will continue to have battles with the flesh.

Job, in the middle of his calamity, marveled that God still thinks of mankind. Job 7:17 says,

> *What is man, that thou shouldest magnify him? and that thou shouldest set thine heart upon him?*

Then again in Job 15:14 he asks,

> *What is man, that he should be clean? and he which is born of a woman, that he should be righteous?*

The Psalmist David asked a similar question found in Psalm 8:4 and 144:3 as seen below.

Psalm 8:4

> *"What is man, that thou art mindful of him? and the son of man, that thou visitest him?"*

Psalm 144:3

"LORD, what is man, that thou takest knowledge of him! or the son of man, that thou makest account of him! "

Doesn't is marvel you that a perfect, holy God like ours loves us? Doesn't it humble you that He would take knowledge of us and be mindful of us? Doesn't it make you to want to live for Him Who has done so much for us in that He sent His Son Jesus to die in our place because He loves us? Why then, should we just flippantly sin and not think a thing about it? Why should we go through our daily walk with hardness and a care-less attitude about our sin and sinfulness? Why?

If we are going to have victory over sin we must recognize what sin is and that even though we are saved, we are sinful creatures. As Paul described his sinful nature, we too must come to grips that we are sinners and that God hates sin and when we sin, **God is not pleased!**

We must first see that we are born sinners. Psalm 51:5 states,

"Behold, I was shapen in iniquity; and in sin did my mother conceive me."

There should be a true repentance of sin, a change of mind about it and a change of direction concerning it. But also in Revelation 3:17 & 18 in writing to the church (Christians) of Laodicea it says,

"Because thou sayest, I am rich, and increased with goods, and have need of nothing; and knowest not that thou art wretched, and miserable, and poor, and blind, and naked:

I counsel thee to buy of me gold tried in the fire, that thou mayest be rich; and white raiment, that thou mayest be clothed, and that the shame of thy nakedness do not appear; and anoint thine eyes with eyesalve, that thou mayest see."

Again, this is written to Christians warning them to open their eyes and see their sinfulness. We see the view from the Christians perspective first in verse 17a and then from God's point of view in the last part of the verse and then what to do about it in verse 18. Open your eyes to your sinfulness Christian!

We all know that a nation is made up of people. It is not just an area; it is an area of people. In referring to Israel in Isaiah 1:4 it says,

> *"Ah sinful nation, a people laden with iniquity, a seed of evildoers, children that are corrupters: they have forsaken the LORD, they have provoked the Holy One of Israel unto anger, they are gone away backward."*

Even though God has a special place for the nation of Israel, He will not excuse their disobedience, He will not excuse their sin and for a nation to get right with Him, the people must admit their sinfulness and turn from their wicked ways. (2 Chronicles 7:14)

In Luke 5:1-7 we see this.

> *"And it came to pass, that, as the people pressed upon him to hear the word of God, he stood by the lake of Gennesaret,*
>
> *And saw two ships standing by the lake: but the fishermen were gone out of them, and were washing their nets.*
>
> *And he entered into one of the ships, which was Simon's, and prayed him that he would thrust out a little from the land. And he sat down, and taught the people out of the ship.*
>
> *Now when he had left speaking, he said unto Simon, Launch out into the deep, and let down your nets for a draught.*
>
> *And Simon answering said unto him, Master, we have toiled all the night, and have taken nothing: nevertheless at thy word I will let down the net.*

> *And when they had this done, they inclosed a great multitude of fishes: and their net brake.*
>
> *And they beckoned unto their partners, which were in the other ship, that they should come and help them. And they came, and filled both the ships, so that they began to sink.*
>
> *When Simon Peter saw it, he fell down at Jesus' knees, saying, Depart from me; for I am a sinful man, O Lord."*

You cannot come into the presence of Jesus without feeling your sinfulness. You also cannot come into His presence without acknowledging your sin!

Psalm 139:23 & 24 says,

> *"Search me, O God, and know my heart: try me, and know my thoughts:*
>
> *And see if there be any wicked way in me, and lead me in the way everlasting."*

In the Lord's Prayer in Luke 11:4 it says,

> *"And forgive us our sins; for we also forgive every one that is indebted to us. And lead us not into temptation; but deliver us from evil."*

When the Prodigal son came to himself he saw his condition and lamented at what he had done and repented and then turned to go back to the father. For us to think we can come to God without a change of mind about sin, which I will say much more about in another chapter, and to think that we can come to a Holy God without trying to get cleaned up is just insane. We get to go to the Father through the righteousness of Jesus Christ, but to be so bold as to go to Him without a change of mind about sin is insanity!

Look at the following verses about the sinfulness of man...

Romans 3:12-18

"They are all gone out of the way, they are together become unprofitable; there is none that doeth good, no, not one.

Their throat is an open sepulchre; with their tongues they have used deceit; the poison of asps is under their lips:

Whose mouth is full of cursing and bitterness:

Their feet are swift to shed blood:

Destruction and misery are in their ways:

And the way of peace have they not known:

There is no fear of God before their eyes."

Romans 8:6-7

"For to be carnally minded is death; but to be spiritually minded is life and peace. Because the carnal mind is enmity against God: for it is not subject to the law of God, neither indeed can be."

Again, we must come to the realization that we are sinners. Though we are not to serve sin, we too have the constant battle between the flesh and the Spirit. We too must admit, as did Paul, that, "…that which I do, I allow not; for what I would that do I not: but what I hate, that I do." (Romans 7:15)

Samuel Bolton said,

"Sin is the practical blasphemy of the name of God. It is the dare of His justice, the rape of His mercy, the slight of His power, the contempt of His love: it is in every way contrary to God!"

The sinfulness of man is emphasized in Genesis 6:5.

"And GOD saw that the wickedness of man was great in the earth, and that every imagination of the thoughts of his heart was only evil continually."

Mankind was so bad that it,

> *"...repented the LORD that he had made man on the earth, and it grieved him at his heart."*

If it was that way then without television, internet pornography, violent games and the movement to reject God in our society, imagine what it must look like today with God which again brings me back to my question, "If our righteousness's look like filthy rags, I wonder what our sins look like?"

Romans 7:24-25

> *"O wretched man that I am! who shall deliver me from the body of this death?*
>
> *I thank God through Jesus Christ our Lord. So then with the mind I myself serve the law of God; but with the flesh the law of sin."*

CHAPTER THREE

What is Sin?

1 John 3:4

"Whosoever committeth sin transgresseth also the law: for sin is the transgression of the law."

Someone once came up with an acrostic for the word "GRACE." It is God's riches at Christ's expense. The grace of God is not a force; it is what God shows us and what He gives us. Grace is God's unmerited favor; it is God giving us what we do not deserve while His mercy is what God does not give us that we do deserve. We are saved by His grace, not by our works. God hates sin enough to send His Son Jesus to die for us. That is His grace!

I have come up with an acrostic for the word "sin." It is, "self-indulgent neglect." Another one is, "self-inflicted negligence." But what is sin? According to the verse above sin is the transgression, or the breaking of the laws of God.

As I taught in Chapter One, the law points us to our need of the Saviour; it shows us we are sinners. 1 Timothy 1:8-11 tells us,

> *"But we know that the law is good, if a man use it lawfully;*
>
> *Knowing this, that the law is not made for a righteous man, but for the lawless and disobedient, for the ungodly and for sinners, for unholy and profane, for murderers of fathers and murderers of mothers, for manslayers,*
>
> *For whoremongers, for them that defile themselves with mankind, for menstealers, for liars, for perjured persons, and if there be any other thing that is contrary to sound doctrine;*

According to the glorious gospel of the blessed God, which was committed to my trust."

Once we see, by the law of God that we are sinners, we then see our need of a Saviour. We are sinners because we sin, or, we are sinners because we are breaking the laws of God since sin is the transgression of the law.

In James 2:8-11 is this…

"If ye fulfil the royal law according to the scripture, Thou shalt love thy neighbour as thyself, ye do well:

But if ye have respect to persons, ye commit sin, and are convinced of the law as transgressors.

For whosoever shall keep the whole law, and yet offend in one point, he is guilty of all.

For he that said, Do not commit adultery, said also, Do not kill. Now if thou commit no adultery, yet if thou kill, thou art become a transgressor of the law."

This shows us WHY we are sinners and to what extent we need to sin or break Gods law in order to BE sinners. I believe verse 10 is the key verse in this and it says, **"For whosoever shall keep the whole law, and yet offend in one point, he is guilty of all."** Though we think we are perfect in all areas, when we break one point of the law, and we all have, we are then sinners because we have sinned.

As we normally quote Romans 3:23 and 5:12 to people while witnessing to them, we emphasize to them that all have sinned, and because all have sinned, we all have the penalty of death. We are sinners because we have transgressed God's law, we have broken the law. Again, in His sight, as it says in Romans 3:10,

"As it is written, There is none righteous, no, not one:"

This leads me then back to my original statement, "If our righteousnesses look like filthy rags, what must our sins look like?"

Sin is the antithesis of holiness. Sin is anything that holiness is not and sin is anything that is diametrically opposed to holiness. In Galatians chapter five we see the works of the flesh and the fruit of the Spirit in comparison; they show us how diametrically opposed sin is to what is holy and right and pleasing in God's sight.

Galatians 5:19-26

"Now the works of the flesh are manifest, which are these; Adultery, fornication, uncleanness, lasciviousness, Idolatry, witchcraft, hatred, variance, emulations, wrath, strife, seditions, heresies, Envyings, murders, drunkenness, revellings, and such like: of the which I tell you before, as I have also told you in time past, that they which do such things shall not inherit the kingdom of God. But the fruit of the Spirit is love, joy, peace, longsuffering, gentleness, goodness, faith, Meekness, temperance: against such there is no law. And they that are Christ's have crucified the flesh with the affections and lusts. If we live in the Spirit, let us also walk in the Spirit. Let us not be desirous of vain glory, provoking one another, envying one another."

In Exodus chapter twenty we have the first specific mention of what we call the Ten Commandments. One of the commandments is, **"Thou shalt not commit adultery."** As you might have noticed in the above verses, one of the works of the flesh is adultery. Many people have not committed actual, physical adultery, but every person has committed mental adultery. Mental adultery? What is that?

Matthew 5:27, 28

"Ye have heard that it was said by them of old time, Thou shalt not commit adultery:

But I say unto you, That whosoever looketh on a woman to lust after her hath committed adultery with her already in his heart."

Anyone who is alive and breathing or who has been alive or who will be alive will commit mental adultery. As a matter of fact much of the advertising world, if not all of it, is based on mental adultery and coveteousness. They advertise using attractive people and cause you to lust or they advertise something someone has and causes you to covet something. They appeal to our sinful nature, the flesh showing once again that we are sinners and that we sin. We do those things and think those things which are contrary to holiness and it is a constant fight between the flesh and the Spirit.

If we are to really see sin and make it exceeding sinful, we should not look at it from our point of view, but from God's! How does He feel about sin? How does He see sin? What did He have to do because of sin?

Now this is where humanism clashes with what I will say because humanism looks at everything from man's point of view, not God's. To a secular humanist, what is wrong to one person is acceptable to another and we are not to impose our beliefs on others. We cannot be dogmatic or judgmental according to them but they forget one very important thing in all their rhetoric and you must remember it too, there is a God in heaven who has a view about sin and what it is and it is His point of view that matters above all others. I will not answer to mankind in eternity; I will answer to God for the things done in my body.

Hebrews 1:9

"Thou hast loved righteousness, and hated iniquity; therefore God, even thy God, hath anointed thee with the oil of gladness above thy fellows. "

Jeremiah 44:4

"Howbeit I sent unto you all my servants the prophets, rising early and sending them, saying, Oh, do not this abominable thing that I hate."

2 Corinthians 5:10

"For we must all appear before the judgment seat of Christ; that every one may receive the things done in his body, according to that he hath done, whether it be good or bad. "

I found this once in my reading and it comes from the Moody Monthly. (I do not know what edition to properly refer you to it.)

What is Sin?

Man calls it an accident; God calls it abomination.

Man calls it a blunder; God calls it blindness.

Man calls it a defect; God calls it a disease.

Man calls it a chance; God calls it a choice.

Man calls it and error; God calls it an enmity.

Man calls it a fascination; God calls it a fatality.

Man calls it a luxury; God calls it leprosy.

Man calls it a liberty; God calls it lawlessness.

Man calls it a trifle; God calls it a tragedy.

Man calls it a mistake; God calls it madness.

Man calls it a weakness; God calls it wickedness!

Our refusal to label sin as sin has led to a society that cannot and does not recognize immorality. They are also confused as to what is good and what is not. They accept homosexuality and condone abortion and then turn around and condemn as terrible things those that are really good things. When God saw the sinfulness of man in Genesis 6:5-6 it says,

"And GOD saw that the wickedness of man was great in the earth, and that every imagination of

the thoughts of his heart was only evil continually.

And it repented the LORD that he had made man on the earth, and it grieved him at his heart."

It actually repented God; it grieved Him that He had made man. His creation of man caused God to grieve because of their sinfulness. Their every imagination of the thoughts of their heart was only evil continually and it grieved Him to the point where He destroyed all living beings except of course for Noah and his immediate family.

Let me give an example of how mankind views a sin and then show how God views that sin. A person whom I know once told me that they know a person who is a homosexual but that the individual was not a pervert. The idea was that since the homosexual did not prey on children then he is not a pervert. The definition of a pervert is as follows from Webster's 1828 dictionary,

> 1. To turn from truth, propriety, or from its proper purpose; to distort from its true use or end; as, to pervert reason by misdirecting it; to pervert the laws by misinterpreting and misapplying them; to pervert justice; to pervert the meaning of an author; to pervert nature; to pervert truth.

> 2. To turn from the right; to corrupt.

Homosexuality is a perversion of how God made man. He NEVER intended for man to be with man or woman to be with woman. When God saw that it was not good for the man to be alone He made Eve to be Adams companion and wife. So, even though this person does not prey on children, he is still a pervert because he changed or perverted the original purpose or design. Mankind justifies and accepts sin because we are sinners but God in this case clearly says concerning homosexuality, or sodomy,

Leviticus 18:22

"Thou shalt not lie with mankind, as with womankind: it is abomination."

Romans 1:18 - 32

For the wrath of God is revealed from heaven against all ungodliness and unrighteousness of men, who hold the truth in unrighteousness;

Because that which may be known of God is manifest in them; for God hath shewed it unto them.

For the invisible things of him from the creation of the world are clearly seen, being understood by the things that are made, even his eternal power and Godhead; so that they are without excuse:

Because that, when they knew God, they glorified him not as God, neither were thankful; but became vain in their imaginations, and their foolish heart was darkened.

Professing themselves to be wise, they became fools,

And changed the glory of the uncorruptible God into an image made like to corruptible man, and to birds, and fourfooted beasts, and creeping things.

Wherefore God also gave them up to uncleanness through the lusts of their own hearts, to dishonour their own bodies between themselves:

Who changed the truth of God into a lie, and worshipped and served the creature more than the Creator, who is blessed for ever. Amen.

For this cause God gave them up unto vile affections: for even their women did change the natural use into that which is against nature:

And likewise also the men, leaving the natural use of the woman, burned in their lust one toward another; men with men working that which is unseemly, and receiving in themselves that recompence of their error which was meet.

And even as they did not like to retain God in their knowledge, God gave them over to a reprobate mind, to do those things which are not convenient;

Being filled with all unrighteousness, fornication, wickedness, covetousness, maliciousness; full of envy, murder, debate, deceit, malignity; whisperers,

Backbiters, haters of God, despiteful, proud, boasters, inventors of evil things, disobedient to parents,

Without understanding, covenantbreakers, without natural affection, implacable, unmerciful:

Who knowing the judgment of God, that they which commit such things are worthy of death, not only do the same, but have pleasure in them that do them."

God says sodomy is an abomination! Man accepts it more and more but God still calls it abomination and one with a reprobate mind! We are never to accept nor justify sin, never!

The word abomination in the Hebrew means, "properly something *disgusting* (morally), that is, (as noun) an *abhorrence*; especially *idolatry* or (concretely) an *idol:* - abominable (custom, thing), abomination." In Webster's dictionary it means,

1. Extreme hatred; detestation.

2. The object of detestation, a common signification in scripture.

The way of the wicked is an abomination to the Lord. Proverbs 15.

3. Hence, defilement, pollution, in a physical sense, or evil doctrines and practices, which are moral defilements, idols and idolatry, are called abominations. The Jews were an abomination to the

Egyptians; and the sacred animals of the Egyptians were an abomination to the Jews. The Roman army is called the abomination of desolation. Mat 24:13. In short, whatever is an object of extreme hatred, is called an abomination.

According to Romans 1:28 God gave them over to a reprobate mind. What does that mean? Again from Webster's it means,

1. Not enduring proof or trial; not of standard purity or fineness; disallowed; rejected.

2. Abandoned in sin; lost to virtue or grace.

3. Abandoned to error, or in apostasy. 2 Timothy 3.

From Strong's Concordance it means,

unapproved, that is, *rejected*; by implication *worthless* (literally or morally): - castaway, rejected, reprobate.

We begin to see then what God thinks of sodomy and what we should think about it. It is a vile, loathsome, wicked and sick sin! I am not writing this to be insensitive but to show what God thinks of a certain sin. I know it is not politically correct and I could be accused of being "homophobic" but as I have said in a message, I would much rather be theologically and Biblically correct than politically correct. One has to do with my views from God's point of view and the other from man's point of view.

Now before you get on your high-horse and think that your sin is not so bad, God hates all sin, including yours! It says of the Lord Jesus in Hebrews 1:9,

"Thou hast loved righteousness, and hated iniquity; therefore God, even thy God, hath anointed thee with the oil of gladness above thy fellows."

God hates sin! There is a partial list of sins in Proverbs 6:16 - 19 of particular sins that God hates.

"These six things doth the LORD hate: yea, seven are an abomination unto him:

A proud look, a lying tongue, and hands that shed innocent blood,

An heart that deviseth wicked imaginations, feet that be swift in running to mischief,

A false witness that speaketh lies, and he that soweth discord among brethren."

Sin is the breaking of God's law. What God says is sin, is sin! God hates sin without respect of persons or nationalities. We who are Christians have one place where we find, according to God, what sin is and what is sin. We are to agree with Him; we are to also have a hatred for sin. The one place where we find what is sin is the Holy Scriptures, the Bible, God's Word. The Bible is the mind of God and all that mankind needs to know about what He considers sin is as found in Scripture.

Sin is everything that is repugnant to God. Sin is what caused death to pass upon all mankind. Sin is our rejection of God and what He says. Sin is direct disobedience to God and all He wrote to us in Scripture. Sin is surrounding the letter "I" in the word sin. Sin causes us to be at odds with God and even ourselves who are made in the image of God. Sin is the blight of all mankind and even nature. Sin leads to nothing but calamity. Sin brings the chastisement and judgment of God. Sin plays into the devils will and against God's. Sin is what caused Adam and Eve to be escorted out of the Garden of Eden. Sin is what caused the cities of Sodom and Gomorrah to be destroyed. Sin is what caused King Saul to lose his position and favor with God. Sin is what caused King David to commit adultery, the murder of Bathsheba's husband and caused his own children to go against their father. Sin is what caused Israel to be put under bondage to Babylon, the Medes and Persians and Rome. Sin is what caused Jesus to be born and then suffer excruciating pain and humility on the cross and ultimately His death. Sin, when it is finished bringeth forth death! Be warned! Sin, though it may be pleasurable for a season, never ends up good!

What good thing does adultery do?

What good thing does liquor or dope do?

What good thing does murder and hatred do?

What good thing does gossip and lies do?

What good thing does any kind of immorality do?

What good thing does pornography do?

What good thing does tobacco do?

Sin is everything that is not holy!

Sin causes death, sometimes immediately!

Sin caused mankind to be expelled from Eden!

Sin caused mankind to be at enmity with God!

Sin caused Jesus, Who knew no sin, to become sin to pay sins penalty!

Sin causes disease! (Job 20:11)

Sin causes separation from God!

Sin causes chastisement!

Sin causes untold misery to individuals, families and even whole nations.

Sin causes a burden for our soul. (Psalm 38:4)

Sin is destructive. (Psalm 34:21)

Sin causes misery. (Psalm 51:3)

Sin is a slap to the face of God.

Sin causes heartache in the one doing it and in those it affects. (The adulterer searches for the precious life and cannot find it. Proverbs 6:26)

There is NOTHING GOOD ABOUT SIN!

Be sure your sin will find you out!

What must our sin look like?

CHAPTER FOUR

The Fight is On!

Romans 7:14-25

"For we know that the law is spiritual: but I am carnal, sold under sin.

For that which I do I allow not: for what I would, that do I not; but what I hate, that do I.

If then I do that which I would not, I consent unto the law that it is good.

Now then it is no more I that do it, but sin that dwelleth in me.

For I know that in me (that is, in my flesh,) dwelleth no good thing: for to will is present with me; but how to perform that which is good I find not.

For the good that I would I do not: but the evil which I would not, that I do.

Now if I do that I would not, it is no more I that do it, but sin that dwelleth in me.

I find then a law, that, when I would do good, evil is present with me.

For I delight in the law of God after the inward man:

But I see another law in my members, warring against the law of my mind, and bringing me into captivity to the law of sin which is in my members.

O wretched man that I am! who shall deliver me from the body of this death?

I thank God through Jesus Christ our Lord. So then with the mind I myself serve the law of God; but with the flesh the law of sin."

Most would consider the Apostle Paul to be the best example of a Christian in the New Testament. He would not agree with that and especially in light of his past before salvation and his personal struggles as a Christian. The purpose of this chapter is to attempt to show the personal struggle that not only Paul had with sin, but how we too have the same struggles and are hindered daily with sin, no matter how "good" of a Christian we are.

Here is Paul's attitude about his personal life.

1 Timothy 1:12-16

"And I thank Christ Jesus our Lord, who hath enabled me, for that he counted me faithful, putting me into the ministry;

Who was before a blasphemer, and a persecutor, and injurious: but I obtained mercy, because I did it ignorantly in unbelief.

And the grace of our Lord was exceeding abundant with faith and love which is in Christ Jesus.

This is a faithful saying, and worthy of all acceptation, that Christ Jesus came into the world to save sinners; of whom I am chief.

Howbeit for this cause I obtained mercy, that in me first Jesus Christ might shew forth all longsuffering, for a pattern to them which should hereafter believe on him to life everlasting."

While we look up to Paul, and well we should, he recognized himself as the "chief of sinners." I believe that if we are to have any kind of victory over sin in our lives, we must always remember that we were born in sin. In Psalm 51:5 the Psalmist, King David, who was described by God as a man after His own heart, wrote,

"Behold, I was shapen in iniquity; and in sin did my mother conceive me."

In Spurgeon's *Treasury of David* it states on this verse,

"He is thunderstruck at the discovery of his inbred sin, and proceeds to set it forth. This was not intended to justify himself, but it rather meant to complete the confession. It is as if he said, not only have I sinned this once, but I am in my very nature a sinner. The fountain of my life is polluted as well as its streams. My birth-tendencies are out of the square of equity; I naturally lean to forbidden things. Mine is a constitutional disease, rendering my very person obnoxious to thy wrath. "*And in sin did my mother conceive me.*" He goes back to the earliest moment of his being, not to traduce his mother, but to acknowledge the deep tap-roots of his sin. It is a wicked wresting of Scripture to deny that original sin and natural depravity are here taught. Surely men who cavil at this doctrine have need to be taught of the Holy Spirit what be the first principles of the faith. David's mother was the Lord's handmaid, he was born in chaste wedlock, of a good father, and he was himself "the man after God's own heart;" and yet his nature was as fallen as that of any other son of Adam, and there only needed the occasion for the manifesting of that sad fact. In our shaping we were put out of shape, and when we were conceived our nature conceived sin. Alas, for poor humanity! Those who will may cry it up, but he is most blessed who in his own soul has learned to lament its lost estate."

In the introduction in my Bible on Psalm 51 telling the circumstances this Psalm was written it says,

"...when Nathan the prophet came unto him (David) after David had gone into Bathsheba."

David, the man after God's own heart, had committed adultery with Bathsheba, he then connived to have her husband killed in battle, and then he had to lie...he had created a mess because of his sin. But Psalm 51 is a prayer of David for forgiveness of all this sin.

Psalm 51:1-19

"Have mercy upon me, O God, according to thy lovingkindness: according unto the multitude of thy tender mercies blot out my transgressions.

Wash me throughly from mine iniquity, and cleanse me from my sin.

For I acknowledge my transgressions: and my sin is ever before me.

Against thee, thee only, have I sinned, and done this evil in thy sight: that thou mightest be justified when thou speakest, and be clear when thou judgest.

Behold, I was shapen in iniquity; and in sin did my mother conceive me.

Behold, thou desirest truth in the inward parts: and in the hidden part thou shalt make me to know wisdom.

Purge me with hyssop, and I shall be clean: wash me, and I shall be whiter than snow.

Make me to hear joy and gladness; that the bones which thou hast broken may rejoice.

Hide thy face from my sins, and blot out all mine iniquities.

Create in me a clean heart, O God; and renew a right spirit within me.

Cast me not away from thy presence; and take not thy holy spirit from me.

Restore unto me the joy of thy salvation; and uphold me with thy free spirit.

Then will I teach transgressors thy ways; and sinners shall be converted unto thee.

Deliver me from bloodguiltiness, O God, thou God of my salvation: and my tongue shall sing aloud of thy righteousness.

O Lord, open thou my lips; and my mouth shall shew forth thy praise.

For thou desirest not sacrifice; else would I give it: thou delightest not in burnt offering.

The sacrifices of God are a broken spirit: a broken and a contrite heart, O God, thou wilt not despise.

Do good in thy good pleasure unto Zion: build thou the walls of Jerusalem

Then shalt thou be pleased with the sacrifices of righteousness, with burnt offering and whole burnt offering: then shall they offer bullocks upon thine altar."

We must always remember that every person has the capability to commit any and all sins. Why? Because we are sinners by our fleshly nature. We all have the sin nature, we were all born in iniquity, and we are all sinners who have come short of the glory of God!

As we remember that we are sinners and what makes us sinners is the breaking of one command of the laws of God, then we must also understand we will always have a battle between our flesh and the Spirit. This is what Romans 7:14 through 25 is all about. I am also going to insert here a **very** important verse.

I Corinthians 10:13 says,

"There hath no temptation taken you but such as is common to man: but God is faithful, who will not suffer you to be tempted above that ye are able; but will with the temptation also make a way to escape, that ye may be able to bear it."

The first thing mentioned in this verse is that "There hath no temptation taken you but such as is common to man..." Temptation and sin are both common to all men. All are tempted to sin, it is common. Sin is common with all mankind; we all have these same battles in life! Satan even tried to tempt Jesus in Matthew 4:1-11 but was without any success at all. In Hebrews 4:15 in his teaching about Jesus Christ it says,

"For we have not an high priest which cannot be touched with the feeling of our infirmities; but was in all points tempted like as we are, yet without sin."

Jesus was tempted like all men are tempted but He never sinned! Look at the following verses too.

Hebrews 7:26, 27

"For such an high priest became us, who is holy, harmless, undefiled, separate from sinners, and made higher than the heavens;

Who needeth not daily, as those high priests, to offer up sacrifice, first for his own sins, and then for the people's: for this he did once, when he offered up himself."

1 Peter 2:21-24

For even hereunto were ye called: because Christ also suffered for us, leaving us an example, that ye should follow his steps:

Who did no sin, neither was guile found in his mouth:

Who, when he was reviled, reviled not again; when he suffered, he threatened not; but committed himself to him that judgeth righteously:

Who his own self bare our sins in his own body on the tree, that we, being dead to sins, should live unto righteousness: by whose stripes ye were healed."

Temptation is common and we will see later how to handle it when tempted to sin.

Paul said in Romans 7:14,

"For we know that the law is spiritual: but I am carnal, sold under sin."

In his teaching in Romans 5:6 & 7 he makes a bold and very honest statement, "I am carnal!" He recognized his humanity; he recognizes his sinful nature even after salvation. We too need to be honest and admit that even as Christians we all struggle with sin! In Psalm 139:23 & 24 the Psalmist wrote,

"Search me, O God, and know my heart: try me, and know my thoughts:

And see if there be any wicked way in me, and lead me in the way everlasting."

I have often said we must be brutally honest with ourselves recognizing our sinful potential and constantly be on guard against sin and especially that sin that doth so easily beset us. We must acknowledge our sinful nature and ask our Father to search us and see if there is any wicked way in us. The fight is on between the flesh and the spirit and we must identify our enemy, the flesh!

This is why we struggle with music! This is why we struggle with our mind and what we listen to and watch to control our mind. There is a constant struggle.

Isn't it true that about the time we feel we have finally defeated that sin that we always fall to that we find ourselves right in the middle of it again! I will show you later how to get control based on one verse, but for now we must recognize that we always have a battle between our flesh and our spirit. We must not only recognize that though we are saved from sins penalty, we are still in our carnal, fleshly body, but we are to also understand that as long as we are in this flesh we will always battle with sin. Paul said in Romans 7:18-20,

"For I know that in me (that is, in my flesh,) dwelleth no good thing: for to will is present with me; but how to perform that which is good I find not.

For the good that I would I do not: but the evil which I would not, that I do.

Now if I do that I would not, it is no more I that do it, but sin that dwelleth in me."

He also made another crucial statement in verse 21 when he stated,

"I find then a law, that, when I would do good, evil is present with me."

We must always be on guard!

When I was in the Navy going through boot camp we always had a guard at each end of the barracks. They were to always stand at ease until an officer came in and the guard was then supposed to snap to attention and say, "Officer on deck!" Everyone in the barracks was to stop what they were doing and stand to attention. Well, one day it was my turn to be on guard duty. I let my guard down and was looking around some and did not notice the officer standing beside me until one of the guys hollered out, "Attention on deck!" I was supposed to holler that and man did I get chewed out and rightly so. That is exactly like sin! You never know when you will be faced with it unless you are planning on sinning, so you had just better always be on guard.....or you will suffer the consequences! When I would do good....evil is present with me!

Paul states it pretty well in summation of this chapter when he wrote,

> *"O wretched man that I am! who shall deliver me from the body of this death?*
>
> *I thank God through Jesus Christ our Lord. So then with the mind I myself serve the law of God; but with the flesh the law of sin."*

Don't let your guard down for a minute! Remember, you will always have a fight between the flesh and the spirit so,

1 Peter 5:8-9

> *"Be sober, be vigilant; because your adversary the devil, as a roaring lion, walketh about, seeking whom he may devour:*
>
> *Whom resist stedfast in the faith, knowing that the same afflictions are accomplished in your brethren that are in the world."*

CHAPTER FIVE

The Judges Cycle

In my personal study of the book of Judges I began to notice certain events that happened over and over again. Since I saw this cycle of events, and since it is in the book of Judges, I named it the "Judges Cycle." I will have you read Judges 4:1-24 to see the basics of this cycle and it will be seen very clearly. First, please read the following verses.

Judges 4:1-24

"And the children of Israel again did evil in the sight of the LORD, when Ehud was dead. And the LORD sold them into the hand of Jabin king of Canaan, that reigned in Hazor; the captain of whose host was Sisera, which dwelt in Harosheth of the Gentiles. And the children of Israel cried unto the LORD: for he had nine hundred chariots of iron; and twenty years he mightily oppressed the children of Israel. And Deborah, a prophetess, the wife of Lapidoth, she judged Israel at that time. And she dwelt under the palm tree of Deborah between Ramah and Bethel in mount Ephraim: and the children of Israel came up to her for judgment. And she sent and called Barak the son of Abinoam out of Kedeshnaphtali, and said unto him, Hath not the LORD God of Israel commanded, saying, Go and draw toward mount Tabor, and take with thee ten thousand men of the children of Naphtali and of the children of Zebulun? And I will draw unto thee to the river Kishon Sisera, the captain of Jabin's army, with his chariots and his multitude; and I will deliver him into thine hand. And Barak said unto her, If thou wilt go with me, then I will go: but if thou wilt not go with me, then I will not go. And she said, I will surely go with thee: notwithstanding the journey that thou takest shall not be for thine honour; for the LORD shall sell Sisera into the hand of a woman. And Deborah arose, and went

with Barak to Kedesh. And Barak called Zebulun and Naphtali to Kedesh; and he went up with ten thousand men at his feet: and Deborah went up with him. Now Heber the Kenite, which was of the children of Hobab the father in law of Moses, had severed himself from the Kenites, and pitched his tent unto the plain of Zaanaim, which is by Kedesh. And they shewed Sisera that Barak the son of Abinoam was gone up to mount Tabor. And Sisera gathered together all his chariots, even nine hundred chariots of iron, and all the people that were with him, from Harosheth of the Gentiles unto the river of Kishon. And Deborah said unto Barak, Up; for this is the day in which the LORD hath delivered Sisera into thine hand: is not the LORD gone out before thee? So Barak went down from mount Tabor, and ten thousand men after him. And the LORD discomfited Sisera, and all his chariots, and all his host, with the edge of the sword before Barak; so that Sisera lighted down off his chariot, and fled away on his feet. But Barak pursued after the chariots, and after the host, unto Harosheth of the Gentiles: and all the host of Sisera fell upon the edge of the sword; and there was not a man left. Howbeit Sisera fled away on his feet to the tent of Jael the wife of Heber the Kenite: for there was peace between Jabin the king of Hazor and the house of Heber the Kenite. And Jael went out to meet Sisera, and said unto him, Turn in, my lord, turn in to me; fear not. And when he had turned in unto her into the tent, she covered him with a mantle. And he said unto her, Give me, I pray thee, a little water to drink; for I am thirsty. And she opened a bottle of milk, and gave him drink, and covered him. Again he said unto her, Stand in the door of the tent, and it shall be, when any man doth come and enquire of thee, and say, Is there any man here? that thou shalt say, No. Then Jael Heber's wife took a nail of the tent, and took an hammer in her hand, and went softly unto him, and smote the nail into his temples, and fastened it into the ground: for he was fast asleep and weary. So he died. And, behold, as Barak pursued Sisera, Jael came out to meet him, and said unto him, Come, and I will shew thee the man whom thou seekest. And when he came into her tent, behold, Sisera lay dead, and the nail was in his temples. So God subdued on that day Jabin the king of Canaan before the children of Israel. And the hand of the children of Israel prospered, and prevailed against Jabin the king of Canaan, until they had destroyed Jabin king of Canaan."

There are basically 6 parts of the Judges Cycle. They are:

1. Whoever is the leader of Israel dies. In Judges 4:1 it says that Ehud the leader dies. Immediately after he died we see the second step in the Judges Cycle.

2. The people immediately go into sin. Again in verse one it tells us, "And the children of Israel again did evil in the sight of the Lord..." We also see this in the following verses. 3:11,12; 6:1; 8:32,33; 12:15 and 13:1

3. After the people go into sin, God punished them in some way, many times by bondage to another nation. Look at Judges 4:2 and 6:1

4. When the people are cast into bondage, they realize what they have done (sinned); they are convicted and repent asking God for another leader or a deliverer. See Judges 4:3

5. God then sends a deliverer (Judge) who leads Israel against the conquering nation and delivers Israel from bondage. See verse 4

6. As long as the Judge is alive, things go well for Israel until he dies then the cycle starts all over again.

How grieved the Father must be with His people! I have already said that as long as we are in this flesh we will have problems with sin. There are those who believe and teach that we cannot sin after salvation, but I think someone forgot to tell Paul that in Romans chapter 7. Fact is, we do sin, we should not, but we do! We are even told in Hebrews to, "...lay aside every weight and the sin which doth so easily beset you." The word "beset" means to surround, to enclose or to hem in. There is a sin or sins, which seems to easily get us! There is little to stop it in our lives it seems. It is there all the time and it is our own fault.

For some, sin, any sin, easily besets them. But, that is another topic. What I want to do in this chapter is look at the Judges Cycle found in the book of Judges to learn from it and to understand then how to stop the vicious cycle in our lives.

First, notice in the first step that the leader dies and the people then immediately go into sin. A fact of life is that EVERYONE NEEDS LEADERSHIP! Everyone needs that influence and that person who helps us in or lives. A child has parents and teachers. A wife has a husband or a boss if they work outside the house. A husband also has a boss or has rules he must abide by if he owns the business. A boss is led by rules of ethics and finances. A Christian must also have leadership in our lives; we need to have a Pastor! Jeremiah 3:12-15 says,

> *"Go and proclaim these words toward the north, and say, Return, thou backsliding Israel, saith the LORD; and I will not cause mine anger to fall upon you: for I am merciful, saith the LORD, and I will not keep anger for ever.*
>
> *Only acknowledge thine iniquity, that thou hast transgressed against the LORD thy God, and hast scattered thy ways to the strangers under every green tree, and ye have not obeyed my voice, saith the LORD.*
>
> *Turn, O backsliding children, saith the LORD; for I am married unto you: and I will take you one of a city, and two of a family, and I will bring you to Zion:*

__And I will give you pastors__ according to mine heart, which shall feed you with knowledge and understanding."

There is always an order or a person in charge and there are followers. The problem is leaders die, retire, or they do something that eliminates them from leadership. In Israel's case during this period of time they did not have a Moses or a Joshua and they had not yet gotten to the point where they had a king. They had Judges who were temporary leaders.

The real test of the depth of your character is what you do when there is no one in charge! For a child, what do you do when mom and dad are not around? What do you do when the teacher is not in the classroom? As an adult, if you travel as I do, how do you act when you are away from your spouse? When in that motel room with the door locked and no one there but yourself, do you watch thing on the television that you would not watch at home? When your wife or husband is not in your office or in the room and you are on the internet, what web site do you look at? Is it pornography? What do you do when the boss leaves the building? What do you do when there is no leader?

What happened with Israel in the book of Judges shows us the sinfulness of man and how quickly we run to sin. We do not know how much time elapsed from the time each leader died to when Israel sinned, but we know it happened. In Judges 3:11 & 12, I want you to look at the wording.

"And the land had rest forty years. And Othniel the son of Kenaz died.

__And the children of Israel did evil again in the sight of the LORD__: and the LORD strengthened Eglon the king of Moab against Israel, because they had done evil in the sight of the LORD."

From there go to Judges 4:1 where it says,

"And the children of Israel __again__ did evil in the sight of the LORD, when Ehud was dead."

Over and over again when there was no leader, the people went into sin, they did that which was against the Lord God…and they always paid for it! Remember, there is always a penalty for sin no matter who you are!

We are all familiar with the event in the life of Moses when he was up on the mountain for 40 days and nights. The people in Exodus 32:1 said,

> *"And when the people saw that Moses delayed to come down out of the mount, the people gathered themselves together unto Aaron, and said unto him, Up, make us gods, which shall go before us; for as for this Moses, the man that brought us up out of the land of Egypt, we wot not what is become of him."*

Then God told Moses in Exodus 32:7 & 8,

> *"And the LORD said unto Moses, Go, get thee down; for thy people, which thou broughtest out of the land of Egypt, have corrupted themselves:*
>
> *Exo 32:8 They have turned <u>aside quickly</u> out of the way which I commanded them: they have made them a molten calf, and have worshipped it, and have sacrificed thereunto, and said, These be thy gods, O Israel, which have brought thee up out of the land of Egypt."*

The point being, when the people thought their leader was dead or gone, they QUICKLY went against God's will, they QUICKLY sinned.

How about another case from Proverbs 29:15b which states,

> *"The rod and reproof give wisdom: but a child left to himself bringeth his mother to shame."*

There is no doubt here that when a child is left alone that they will do that which is against their parents teaching. They will bring their mother to shame. Again, no leader around, we go head-long into sin!

From the point when the leader dies the people quickly go into sin, we see the next part which is after the people go into sin; God's punishment comes on the people.

To properly understand how God feels about sin, I once again refer you to Hebrews 1:8 which tells us that God HATES INIQUITY! Sin caused the removal of Lucifer and all the "fallen" angels from heaven and caused the existence of hell since it was made for the devil and his angels. (Matthew 25:41) Sin caused death! But most importantly sin is what caused a Holy God to send His only begotten Son Jesus to die for our sins. Notice too the attitude of Jesus about what sin did to Him as found in Hebrews 12:2 where it says that Jesus…"endured the cross, despising the shame." In 2 Corinthians 5:21 it says,

> *"For he hath made him to be sin for us, who knew no sin; that we might be made the righteousness of God in him."*

Jesus never sinned yet He BECAME sin for us and the righteous Jesus suffered for our sin! Sin has a penalty!

In Isaiah 53:4-6 it says,

> *"Surely he hath borne our griefs, and carried our sorrows: yet we did esteem him stricken, smitten of God, and afflicted.*
>
> *But he was wounded for our transgressions, he was bruised for our iniquities: the chastisement of our peace was upon him; and with his stripes we are healed.*
>
> *All we like sheep have gone astray; we have turned every one to his own way; and the LORD hath laid on him the iniquity of us all."*

How great is the grace and mercy of our God, yet how righteous are His judgments on sin! But, in all this we must remember there is always a punishment for and because of sin! Ultimately, the wages of sin is death, but we must also remember in Hebrews 12:5-7 it says,

"And ye have forgotten the exhortation which speaketh unto you as unto children, My son, despise not thou the chastening of the Lord, nor faint when thou art rebuked of him:

For whom the Lord loveth he chasteneth, and scourgeth every son whom he receiveth.

If ye endure chastening, God dealeth with you as with sons; for what son is he whom the father chasteneth not?"

We must not forget the principle of reaping and sowing! Galatians 6:7-8 says,

"Be not deceived; God is not mocked: for whatsoever a man soweth, that shall he also reap.

For he that soweth to his flesh shall of the flesh reap corruption; but he that soweth to the Spirit shall of the Spirit reap life everlasting."

John Gill wrote on this verse,

"Be not deceived,.... By false teachers, who, in order to engross all to themselves, dissuaded the Galatians from communicating to their honourable pastors, and faithful ministers of the word; or by themselves, who being of a tenacious and covetous disposition, devised various things to excuse them from performing this their duty to the preachers of the Gospel; as that they had families of their own to maintain, that their circumstances were such that they could give little or nothing this way, and the others, who were of better abilities in life, ought to bear this charge; and with such like things endeavoured to satisfy their consciences in the neglect of their duty: but this was all self-deception, for

God is not mocked; nor will he be; men may deceive themselves, and others, with such excuses and false appearances, yet they cannot deceive God, who knows their hearts as well as their worldly substance, and that the omission of their duty arises not from want of ability, but from a covetous temper; and who looks upon withholding from his ministers that which is due unto them as mocking of him, and which he will not suffer with impunity: for whatsoever a man soweth, that shall he also reap; as to kind, quality, and quantity, generally speaking; if he sows wheat he reaps wheat, if he sows barley he reaps barley; no man can expect to reap another sort than what he sows; and if it is good seed he may hope for a good crop; and if he sows bountifully, he shall reap bountifully; but if he sows sparingly, he shall reap sparingly; and if he sows nothing, he can never reap anything. This is a proverbial expression, and may be applied to all actions, good and bad, and the reward and punishment of them, and particularly to acts of beneficence, and the enjoying of the fruits thereof."

When God told Israel in Deuteronomy 11:26-28 that there was a blessing if they obeyed the commands of God and a curse if they did not, He was telling them that they would reap what they sowed! Whatsoever a man sows, that shall he reap! You cannot sow sin and reap blessings! If we sow of the flesh, we shall reap of the flesh! Simple as that!

In the Judges cycle we see the chastisement upon the people because of sin! Another thing to remember is who the Lord loves, He chastises as we saw earlier.

God NEVER allows sin to be gotten away with...NEVER! This is one of the problems in today's society and it begins in the house of God! Because of our lax view of sin, it has become more and more practiced and allowed. Because there is a looseness on sin from within Christianity, there is a growth of sin in society BUT GOD WILL NOT ALLOW IT TO CONTINUE WITHOUT CHASTISEMENT UPON HIS CHILDREN! The nation of Israel went into hundreds of years of bondage, and other forms of punishment mentioned in Scripture, and how shall we escape?

The next step in the Judges cycle should have happened earlier in the cycle, but it seems it never does. Let's look at the steps up to now.

1. The leader dies,

2. The people go into sin,

3. God punishes them, then...

They cry out to God for forgiveness and another leader! My question is, WHY WAIT until you have God's punishment before you cry out to God? Why not cry out to God even before you sin? But, many times we do not repent until we are being chastened. (I will deal with true Biblical repentance later.)

A great thing about God is that when we do the right thing through prayer....He hears us just like He did with Israel in Judges. The formula is found in the famous and oft used verse, 2 Chronicles 7:14. But, sin is so powerful and devastating; it should be repented of IMMEDIATELY! We should not wait because when we do not take care of things immediately, they only get worse. Yes, when we are without leadership, we should pray and watch to refrain from sin and not wait.

When the people pray for this forgiveness and for a leader, God sends them one and they regain their identity as long as the leader is alive....but, when he dies, the whole cycle starts all over again. It is called the sin nature of man and must be guarded against. If you know someone is going to break into your house, you take the necessary steps to protect yourself and your property. Likewise we must be vigilant for, "...your adversary the devil, as a roaring lion, walketh about, seeking whom he may devour. " (1 Peter 5:8) We must be on guard at all times!

We must also remember that when there is no human leadership Jesus Christ promised that He would never leave us or forsake us. (Hebrews 13:5) WE always have the presence of the Holy Spirit with us, He is always there and will lead us if few are sensitive to His leading and He will NOT lead us into sin! We are never truly without leadership in our lives as Christians, but we can so resist His leadership that though He is with us we will not yield to nor feel His leadership in our lives. This is one reason why we doubt our salvation as mentioned already. We doubt our salvation either because we are not saved, or because we are being disobedient. We know that we know Him if we obey Him. (1 John 2:3)

We must understand that we are never truly without leadership even when it seems that we are. Therefore, we must learn and cultivate a dependency upon HIS constant leadership and we must learn to pray and develop a closeness to our Father to always sense His presence in our lives. A great part of the Great Commission is that he promises us, "...lo, I am with you always, even unto the end of the world. Amen!" (Matthew 28:20) Break the vicious Judges cycle!

CHAPTER SIX

It Is Not God's Fault!

James 1:12-25

"Blessed is the man that endureth temptation: for when he is tried, he shall receive the crown of life, which the Lord hath promised to them that love him. Let no man say when he is tempted, I am tempted of God: for God cannot be tempted with evil, neither tempteth he any man: But every man is tempted, when he is drawn away of his own lust, and enticed. Then when lust hath conceived, it bringeth forth sin: and sin, when it is finished, bringeth forth death. Do not err, my beloved brethren. Every good gift and every perfect gift is from above, and cometh down from the Father of lights, with whom is no variableness, neither shadow of turning. Of his own will begat he us with the word of truth, that we should be a kind of firstfruits of his creatures. Wherefore, my beloved brethren, let every man be swift to hear, slow to speak, slow to wrath: For the wrath of man worketh not the righteousness of God. Wherefore lay apart all filthiness and superfluity of naughtiness, and receive with meekness the engrafted word, which is able to save your souls. But be ye doers of the word, and not hearers only, deceiving your own selves. For if any be a hearer of the word, and not a doer, he is like unto a man beholding his natural face in a glass: For he beholdeth himself, and goeth his way, and straightway forgetteth what manner of man he was. But whoso looketh into the perfect law of liberty, and continueth therein, he being not a forgetful hearer, but a doer of the work, this man shall be blessed in his deed. "

We have all made incorrect and even sometimes hateful and hurtful statements for which we will answer. (Matthew 12:35-37) I believe also that those of us who preach and teach from the Scriptures will answer more severely for our unscriptural statements. I have heard many, many strange and, simply put, heretical statements and false doctrine preach from those who should have known better. I even have two large file folders of studies I have made all motivated by making sure that what I heard was accurate or not. Sad to say, many times, yea, most of the time what I heard was not sound doctrine and even sometimes "preached" based on personal abuse of Scripture in order to "get at someone." It seems that those who scream the loudest about the inspiration of the Scriptures are most guilty of abusing them in order to suit their own personal purpose. But, then the Holy Spirit has pointed out that I too have been guilty of being incorrect at times. (Let him who is without sin be the first to throw a stone.)

One of the kinds of statements that people make which goes clearly against Scripture has to do with Gods tempting us with sin in order to see how we will respond. In the above verses there are four very clear places which deal specifically with temptation, sin and who does not tempt us to sin. Let's look at these four verses.

James 1:12

"Blessed is the man that endureth temptation: for when he is tried, he shall receive the crown of life, which the Lord hath promised to them that love him."

The first thing that must be understood are the two kinds of temptation being spoken of here in James 1:12-25.

From the notes of John Gill in his Exposition of the Whole Bible on James 1:2 it says,

> "My brethren,.... Not only according to the flesh, he being a Jew as they were; but in a spiritual sense, they being born again of the same grace, belonging

to the same family and household of faith, and having the same Father, and being all the children of God, by faith in Christ Jesus: count it all joy when ye fall into divers temptations; **not the temptations of Satan, or temptations to sin; for these cannot be matter of joy, but grief; these are fiery darts, and give a great deal of uneasiness and trouble; but afflictions and persecutions for the sake of the Gospel, which are so called here and elsewhere, because they are trials of the faith of God's people, and of other graces of the Spirit of God.** God by these tempts his people, as he did Abraham, when he called him to sacrifice his son; he thereby tried his faith, fear, love, and obedience; so by afflictions, God tries the graces of his people; not that he might know them, for he is not ignorant of them, but that they might be made manifest to others; and these are "divers": many are the afflictions of the righteous; through much tribulation they must enter the kingdom; it is a great fight of afflictions which they endure, as these believers did; their trials came from different quarters; they were persecuted by their countrymen the Jews, and were distressed by the Gentiles, among whom they lived; and their indignities and reproaches were many; and their sufferings of different sorts, as confiscation of goods, imprisonment of body, banishment, scourgings, and death in various shapes: and these they "fall" into; not by chance, nor altogether at an unawares, or unexpectedly; but they fell into them through the wickedness and malice of their enemies, and did not bring them upon themselves through any crime or enormity they were guilty of: and when this was their case, the apostle exhorts them to count it all joy, or matter of joy, of exceeding great joy, even of the greatest joy; not that these afflictions were joyous in themselves, but in their circumstances, effects, and consequences; as they tried, and exercised, and improved the graces of the Spirit, and worked for their good, spiritual and eternal, and produced in them the peaceable fruit of righteousness; and as they were attended with the presence and Spirit of God, and of glory; and as they made for, and issued in the glory of

God; and because of that great reward in heaven which would follow them; see Mat_5:11. The Jews have a saying (g), "whoever rejoices in afflictions that come upon him, brings salvation to the world."

Then in James 1:12 he wrote,

"Blessed is the man that endureth temptation,.... Or affliction, which is designed by temptation, as in Jam_1:2 and the man that endures it is he that so bears it, and bears up under it, as not to be offended at it, and stumble in the ways of Christ, and fall away from the truth, and a profession of it, as temporary believers in a time of temptation do; but manfully and bravely stands up under it, and does not sink under the weight of it, or faint on account of it; and endures afflictions in such manner as not to murmur and repine at them, but is quiet and still, and bears them patiently and constantly, and so endures to the end. Such expect afflictions, and when they come, they are not moved by them, but, notwithstanding them, continue in the ways and work of the Lord; and such are happy persons; they are happy now, and shall be hereafter. Saints are happy under afflictions, and even on account of them, for they are tokens of God's love to them, and evidences of their sonship; and especially they are happy under them, when they enjoy the presence of God in them, when they are instructive to them, and are saner, lifted, when they learn from them the useful lessons of faith, patience, humility, and resignation to the will of God, and are made more partakers of his holiness; and they will be happy hereafter, as follows. The Jews have a saying (h) much like this,

"blessed" is the man, שהוא עומד בנסיונו, "who stands in his temptation", for there is no creature whom the holy blessed God does not tempt."

For when he is tried; by the fire of afflictions, as gold is tried in the fire; when God hereby has tried what is in his heart, and the truth of grace in him, as faith, love, patience, &c. and has purged away his dross and tin, and has refined and purified him, as gold and silver are refined and purified in the furnace, or refining pot: and when being thus tried and proved, and found genuine, and comes forth as gold, after this state of temptation and affliction is over, he shall receive the crown of life, eternal happiness, called a "crown", because of the glory of it, which will be both upon the bodies and souls of believers to all eternity; and as suitable to their character, they being kings, and having a kingdom and thrones prepared for them; and in allusion to the crown that was given to the conquerors in the Olympic games: and it is called a "crown of life", because it is for life, which an earthly crown is not always; and because it lies in eternal life, and is an everlasting crown; it is a crown of glory that fadeth not away, an incorruptible one; and differs from the corruptible crown given to the victors in the above mentioned games, which were made of fading herbs, and leaves of trees: and now the man that bears up under afflictions, and holds out unto the end, shall have this crown put upon him, and he shall "receive it"; not as merited by him, by his works or sufferings, for neither of them are worthy to be compared or mentioned with this crown of life and glory; but as the free gift of God, as it will be given him by the righteous Judge, as a reward of grace, and not of debt: which the Lord hath promised to them that love him; either the Lord Jesus Christ, as in Mat 5:10 or else God the Father; the Vulgate Latin, Syriac, and Ethiopic versions, read, "God"; and the Alexandrian copy leaves out the word "Lord", which may be supplied by the word God; see Jam 2:5 and this promise he made before the world was, who cannot lie, nor deceive, and who is able to perform, and is faithful, and will never suffer his faithfulness to fail; so that this happiness is certain, and may be depended upon: besides, the promise of this crown of life is in Christ, where all the promises are yea and amen; yea, the crown itself is in his hands, where it lies safe and secure for "them that love him"; either the Lord Jesus Christ, his person, his people, his truths, and ordinances, and his glorious appearing, 2Ti 4:8 or God the Father; not that their love is the cause of this crown of life, or eternal life, for then it would not be the free gift of God, as it is said to be; nor of the promise of it, for that was made before the world was, and when they had no love unto him; but this phrase is descriptive of the persons to whom God manifests his love now, admits to near communion and fellowship with himself, makes all things, even their afflictions, to work for their good, and whom he will cause to inherit substance, and will fill their treasures."

It is clear that there are two types of temptations spoken of in these verses. One is the type of temptation where our faith is tried, the other is a temptation to sin. One God allows in our lives to strengthen us, the other is brought on by Satan. Gill said it correctly when he wrote, **"...not the temptations of Satan, or temptations to sin; for these cannot be matter of joy, but grief; these are fiery darts, and give a great deal of uneasiness and trouble; but afflictions and persecutions for the sake of the Gospel, which are so called here and elsewhere, because they are trials of the faith of God's people, and of other graces of the Spirit of God."**

While I was teaching a college class, I illustrated being tempted this way. Everyone knew there was a test coming which was a large part of their final grade. How well they knew the material would determine how well they would do on the test. It would determine whether they would pass or fail the test.

When God has a testing or temptation to come into our lives, it is an opportunity for us to use the information we have gathered from Scripture to help us pass the test. I detest the statement, "God allows temptation of sin to come into our lives to SEE how we will respond." Like He does not know ahead of time how we will respond. He does not have to SEE how we will respond, **HE ALREADY KNOWS!** I am thankful that He knows and, as it is pointed out in 1 Corinthians 10:13, He will not allow us to be tempted above that which we can handle. There are 5 parts to 1 Corinthian 10:13 and they are...

1. Everyone is tempted, it is common with every man,
2. God is faithful in that,

3. He will not suffer or allow us to be tempted above that ye are able,
4. But beside the temptation will make a way to escape that temptation
5. That we will be able to bear or be victorious over it.

God does not just let any and all temptations come our way and He does not allow it to SEE how we will respond; He limits it according to our ability and he will with the temptation also make a way to escape. He is all providing, but we must do our part which is to respond in such a way as to glorify Him. But all of this has little to do with sin.

Back to James 1:13 which clearly states,

"Let no man say when he is tempted, I am tempted of God: for God cannot be tempted with evil, neither tempteth he any man:"

The temptation being spoken of here is not just a testing of our faith; it is talking about being tempted with sin! This is a totally different type of testing which leads to totally different results.

The first temptation led to, "…he shall receive the crown of life." This one in connection with evil and sin leads to death. One builds and is gloriously rewarded; the other destroys and leads to death. If I fail a testing or trial of my faith through persecution, it does not normally lead to death, but to a weaker walk. But a failing to resist temptation to sin leads to death. The question is, who tempts and who does not!

In verse 13 it very clearly says that it is not God Who tempts us with evil! This is dramatically opposed to some who say that, for example, it was God's will that a child's parents got divorced to make that child stronger. This is just simply not true and is not sound doctrine! I even heard an Evangelist say that it was not God's will that his parents got divorced because God knew that he was not strong enough to take it, but that other young people were strong enough to take it and it was God's will that their parents divorced. Since when is it ever God's will that anyone divorces?!

Jesus taught against divorce in Matthew 19:3-9. Then to say it was God's will to get divorced is not at all compatible with the clear teachings of Scripture. If that were true, then all sin would have to be in God's will BUT THIS GOES AGAINST NOT ONLY THE NATURE OF GOD, BUT THE CLEAR VERSE IN JAMES WHICH SAYS, **"LET NO MAN SAY WHEN HE IS TEMPTED (TO SIN), I AM TEMPTED OF GOD; (WHY?) FOR GOD CANNOT BE TEMPTED WITH EVIL, *NEITHER TEMPTETH HE ANY MAN!***

"But," you say, "God allowed it like He did in Job's life, therefore it must have been His will!" That is not good logic at all. God also allows people to die and go to hell, yet that is not His will! Is it His will because He allowed it? Was that God's will for that person? To a hyper-Calvinist the answer would be yes, but what does the Scripture say?

2 Peter 3:9

> *The Lord is not slack concerning his promise, as some men count slackness; but is longsuffering to us-ward, not willing that any should perish, but that all should come to repentance.*

Just because something happens does not make it His will, especially when we are talking about sins! Look at James 1:13 again!

> *Let no man say when he is tempted, I am tempted of God: for God cannot be tempted with evil, <u>neither tempteth he any man:</u>*

DO NOT BLAME GOD FOR YOUR SIN! IT IS NOT HIS FAULT! So, who do we blame?

James 1:14

But every man is tempted, when he is drawn away of his own lust, and enticed.

So who do we blame since it is not God Who tempts us with evil? The temptation that leads to evil is brought on by our own lust! The Devil did not even make you do it, you and I sin because we want to! You yield to the temptation yourself and have no one to blame but yourself! It is not God's fault! It is NEVER His will that we sin and He does not tempt us with evil! He does not tempt us with pornography to see if we will resist it, that was you who did that! Whether you sin or not depends on who you yield your members to according to Romans 6:13 and 19!

Romans 6:13

"Neither yield ye your members as instruments of unrighteousness unto sin: but yield yourselves unto God, as those that are alive from the dead, and your members as instruments of righteousness unto God."

Romans 6:19

"I speak after the manner of men because of the infirmity of your flesh: for as ye have yielded your members servants to uncleanness and to iniquity unto iniquity; even so now yield your members servants to righteousness unto holiness."

We must quit blaming God and everyone else for our sin; we must blame ourselves and say, I have sinned! It is not God's fault you sinned you yielded to your flesh, you lost that battle between the flesh and the Spirit mentioned in a previous chapter. You failed the test!

Proverbs 28:13

He that covereth his sins shall not prosper: but whoso confesseth and forsaketh them shall have mercy.

CHAPTER SEVEN

What Fruit?

Galatians 6:7 - 8

"Be not deceived; God is not mocked: for whatsoever a man soweth, that shall he also reap. For he that soweth to his flesh shall of the flesh reap corruption; but he that soweth to the Spirit shall of the Spirit reap life everlasting."

Romans 6:21

"What fruit had ye then in those things whereof ye are now ashamed? for the end of those things is death."

To make sin exceeding sinful we must look at sin, not from a man's point of view, but from God's. The ever recurring theme of this book is in my question, "If our righteousness to God looks like filthy rags, what must our sins look like?" John Gill wrote concerning Isaiah 64:6,

> "But we are all as an unclean thing,.... Or "we have been" (t); so all men are in a state of nature: man was made pure and holy, but by sinning became impure; and this impurity is propagated by natural generation, and belongs to all, none are free from it; and there is no cleansing from it but by the grace of God and blood of Christ: all are not sensible of it; some are, as the church here was, and owns it, and the universality of it, and compares herself and members to an "unclean thing", on account of it; so men, defiled with sin, are compared to unclean creatures, dogs, and swine, and to unclean persons; to such as are covered with loathsome diseases, and particularly to leprous persons, and who may be chiefly intended here; they being defiled and defiling, loathsome and abominable, their disease spreading and continuing, and incurable by physicians; hence they were separated from the company of men; and the words may be rendered, "as an unclean person"

(u), as such were by the law: or we are, in our own sense and apprehension of things; and this may respect not only the impurity of nature, but a general corruption in doctrine and manners among the professors of religion; such as was in the Jewish church about the time of Christ's coming.

And all our righteousnesses are as filthy rags; which is to be understood not of the righteousness of some persons in the church, which lay in outward rites, ceremonies, and sacrifices, which were no righteousness before God, and could not take away sin; and were indeed on many accounts, as they were performed, loathsome and abominable; see Isa 1:11, or of others that lay in outward legal duties and works of the law, which were not done from right principles, as well as not perfect; and so, because of the impurity, imperfection, pride, and vanity, that appeared in them, were abominable to the Lord: but of the righteousnesses of the church herself; not of the righteousness of Christ, which was made hers by imputation; for this is not rags, but a robe, the best robe, and wedding garment; much less filthy, but pure and spotless, beautiful and glorious, as well as a proper covering; but then, though this is the church's, and all true believers', by gift, by imputation and application, yet its is properly Christ's and is in him, and is opposed to their own righteousness; which is what is intended here, even the best of it; such works of righteousness as are done by them in the best manner; they are "rags", not whole, but imperfect, not fit to appear in before God, and by which they cannot be justified in his sight; they are "filthy" ones, being attended with imperfection and sin; and these conversation garments need continual washing in the blood of Jesus; this is the language not of a natural man, or of a Pharisee, but of a sensible sinner, a truly gracious soul. The words may be rendered, "as a menstruous cloth" (w), as some; or "as a garment of spoil or prey" (x), as Aben Ezra, rolled in blood, either in war, or by a beast of prey; or as a foul plaster or cloth taken off a sore, with purulent matter on it (y), as others; or any other impure and nauseous thing. Hottinger (z) thinks the word has some affinity with the Arabic עדר, which signifies "running water", such as the water of a fountain or well; so that the sense may be, that the church's righteousness was like a cloth, so polluted and spotted that it could not be washed out clean but with clear and running water; and, in every sense in which it may be taken, it serves to set forth the impurity and imperfection of the best righteousness of men, and to show that their works are not the cause of salvation, the church had an assurance of in the preceding verse:

and we all do fade as a leaf; or "fall" (a) as one; as leaves in autumn: this is to be understood of a great part, and perhaps of the greater part, of the visible members of the church; not of true believers and real members, for these are rooted in the love of God, and in Christ, and have the root of the matter in them, the true grace of God; and therefore, though they meet with many blustering storms, yet do not cast their leaf of profession; indeed there may be, as there often are, decays and declensions in them; but rather this is to be interpreted of carnal professors, with which, at this time, the church abounded, who had no true grace in them; and so dropped their profession, and became like trees whose fruit withered, were without fruit; or like trees, in the fall of the year, which are without fruit, and shed their leaves, Jud 1:12,

and our iniquities, like the wind, have taken us away; as a leaf falling from the tree is carried away with the wind, which it is not able to withstand; so formal and carnal professors are carried away, through their sins, with the wind of persecution, and apostatize: or rather for their sins the Jews were carried captive, as before, to Babylon; so now by the Romans into various countries, where they are dispersed at this day; to which this passage may have some respect. "Iniquities" are put for the punishment of them; so the Targum, "and, because of our sins, as the wind we are taken away."

If the best that we can do looks like "menstrous or filthy rags," what must our sin look like?! We cannot even begin to imagine what one sin looks like to a holy God. Look at the following verses to get an idea of how God hates sin.

Deuteronomy 25:16

"For all that do such things, and all that do unrighteously, are an abomination unto the LORD thy God."

2 Samuel 11:27

"And when the mourning was past, David sent and fetched her to his house, and she became his wife, and bare him a son. But the thing that David had done displeased the LORD."

Psalms 5:4

"For thou art not a God that hath pleasure in wickedness: neither shall evil dwell with thee. Psa 5:4 For thou art not a God that hath pleasure in wickedness: neither shall evil dwell with thee."

Psalms 11:5

"The LORD trieth the righteous: but the wicked and him that loveth violence his soul hateth."

Proverbs 6:16-19

"These six things doth the LORD hate: yea, seven are an abomination unto him: A proud look, a lying tongue, and hands that shed innocent blood,

An heart that deviseth wicked imaginations, feet that be swift in running to mischief, A false witness that speaketh lies, and he that soweth discord among brethren."

Zechariah 8:17

"And let none of you imagine evil in your hearts against his neighbour; and love no false oath: for all these are things that I hate, saith the LORD."

Luke 16:15

"And he said unto them, Ye are they which justify yourselves before men; but God knoweth your hearts: for that which is highly esteemed among men is abomination in the sight of God."

Also, in order to make sin exceeding sinful, we must see the results of sin, which, I believe, is why Paul asked the Christians in Romans 6:21,

<u>*What fruit had ye then in those things whereof ye are now ashamed?*</u> *for the end of those things is death.*

First let's look at what "fruit" is in Scripture. There are a few ways fruit is used in Scripture but mainly fruit is used to indicate what comes out of our lives and there are only two kinds of fruit which are "good" fruit and "bad" fruit. The same is true in nature which is what Jesus taught in Matthew 7:17-19.

"Even so every good tree bringeth forth good fruit; but a corrupt tree bringeth forth evil fruit. A good tree cannot bring forth evil fruit, neither can a corrupt tree bring forth good fruit. Every tree that bringeth not forth good fruit is hewn down, and cast into the fire."

We also see the phrase "meet for repentance" two times. Once by John the Baptist in Matthew 3:8 when he said,

"Bring forth therefore fruits meet for repentance:"

and the other by Paul in Act 26:20 where he said,

"But shewed first unto them of Damascus, and at Jerusalem, and throughout all the coasts of Judaea, and then to the Gentiles, that they should repent and turn to God, and do works meet for repentance."

It is obvious that fruit and works are compatible, or, they are talking about the same thing. John Gill wrote concerning Acts 26:20,

"But showed first unto them of Damascus,.... The Jews at Damascus to whom the apostle first preached; see Act 9:20. and at Jerusalem, and throughout all the coasts of Judea; observing the order of his mission, Act 26:17 though it was not until after he had been in Arabia, and had returned to Damascus, that he went to Jerusalem, and preached there; see Gal 1:17 compared with Act 9:28. and then to the Gentiles; as at Antioch in Pisidia, at Iconium, Derbe, and Lystra in Lycaonia; and at Philippi, Thessalonica, and Berea in Macedonia; and in many places in Greece and Asia, as at Athens, Corinth, Ephesus, and others, as this history shows; and indeed he preached the Gospel from Jerusalem round about to Illyricum; that they should repent; that is, that they should repent of their sins; of sin in general, as it is committed against God, is a transgression of his law, and as it is in itself exceeding sinful, and in its effects dreadful; and of particular sins, such as men have been more especially addicted to, and of which the Jews and Gentiles, the apostle was sent unto, and to whom he preached, had been guilty: as the former of their will worship, and following the commandments and traditions of men, thereby making void the law of God; of their rejection and crucifixion of the Messiah; of their persecution of his apostles, ministers, and people; and of their trust in, and dependence upon, their own righteousness for justification: and the latter of their immoralities, superstition, and idolatry; and both not of the outward gross actions of life only, but of inward sins and lusts: and repentance of each of these lies in a different sentiment of them; in a detestation and abhorrence of them; in shame and confusion on account of them; in self-reflections upon them, and humiliation for them; in an ingenuous acknowledgment of them, and turning from them: and this is not a national repentance which the ministers of the Gospel are to show to men the necessity of; though this is not unworthy of them, when there is a call in Providence to it, and the state of things require it; much less a legal one, but an evangelical repentance; which has along with it faith in Christ Jesus, dealing with his blood and righteousness for the remission of their sins, and their justification before God; and which springs from, and is encouraged and heightened by, a sense of the love of God: and now this being a part of the Gospel ministry, does not suppose it to be in the power of men to repent of themselves, since no man, whilst he remains insensible of the evil nature of sin, and the hardness of his heart continues, which none but God can remove, can repent; and when he becomes truly sensible, he then prays to God to give him repentance, and to turn him: nor does it at all contradict its being a blessing of the covenant, a gift of Christ, and a grace of the Spirit of God; nor does it suggest, that the preaching of the word is sufficient of itself to produce it; the contrary of which the ministry of John the Baptist, of Christ, and of his apostles, declares; but the design of its being insisted on in the Gospel ministry, is to show that men are sinners, and in such a state and condition, that they are in need of repentance, and that without it they must perish; and the rather this is to be quietly inculcated, since true repentance is unto life, is the beginning and evidence of spiritual life, and issues in eternal life; and since there is a close connection between that and salvation, and that without it there is no salvation. It follows, and turn to God; this is to be understood, not of the first work of conversion, which is God's work, and not man's act, and in which man is passive, and which is before repentance, whereas this follows upon it; though the ministers of the word have a concern with this; to bring about this is the design and use of their ministrations; their business is to show the nature of conversion, what it is, and wherein it lies; to rectify mistakes about it, and to observe the necessity of it: but here is designed a turning to God, in consequence of the grace of first conversion; by an acknowledgment and confession of sin to God, by an application to him for pardoning grace and mercy, by a trust and dependence on him for righteousness, life, and salvation, and by obedience to his commands and ordinances. It intends a turning of the Jews from their evil principles and practices, from the traditions of their elders to the law of God, the Gospel of Christ, and the ordinances of it, and of the Gentiles, from their idols to the worship of the true and living God: and do works meet for repentance the same with "fruits meet for repentance", Mat 3:8. And such as are particularly mentioned in 2Co 7:11 they are they which are the reverse of the evil actions they have been guilty of, and which are properly good works. And they are they which are done according to the will of God declared in his word, this is a requisite of a good work; what is not according to the word of God is not a good work, nor can it be any evidence of repentance; and they are also such as spring from love to God, for if they are done through fear of punishment, or for sinister and selfish ends, they show repentance to be a mere legal one: and they are such as are done in faith, in the name and strength of Christ, and to the glory of God by him. All external good works are designed, which show that the inward repentance professed, and that the outward change made in religion and worship, are genuine and sincere: the doctrines of internal repentance and outward worship, and all good works, are parts of the Gospel ministry, and to be insisted on in their proper places."

Titus 3:14 equates being fruitful with good works. So fruit in this case equals our works, again being good works. I must pause here and say that there are more good works than winning a person to Christ which is what many equate the word fruit to and only to that it seems. Soul winning is a fruit, but not the only fruit a Christian is to bear. Look at Galatians 5:15-26 quickly.

"But if ye bite and devour one another, take heed that ye be not consumed one of another. This I say then, Walk in the Spirit, and ye shall not fulfil the lust of the flesh. For the flesh lusteth against the Spirit, and the Spirit against the flesh: and these are contrary the one to the other: so that ye cannot do the things that ye would. But if ye be led of the Spirit, ye are not under the law. Now the works of the flesh are manifest, which are these; Adultery, fornication, uncleanness, lasciviousness, Idolatry, witchcraft, hatred, variance,

> *emulations, wrath, strife, seditions, heresies, Envyings, murders, drunkenness, revellings, and such like: of the which I tell you before, as I have also told you in time past, that they which do such things shall not inherit the kingdom of God. But the fruit of the Spirit is love, joy, peace, longsuffering, gentleness, goodness, faith, Meekness, temperance: against such there is no law. And they that are Christ's have crucified the flesh with the affections and lusts. If we live in the Spirit, let us also walk in the Spirit. Let us not be desirous of vain glory, provoking one another, envying one another."*

The fruit of the Spirit is what is to come out of us just like oranges come from orange trees.

John 15:1-16 has been taught primarily in the past as the fruit being souls for Christ. Again, that is **A** fruit of the Christian, but not the only one. As we saw before fruit equals works, good and bad. Naturally then, in looking at John 15 it is not just talking about soul winning, but bearing good fruit, or, having good works. Our Fathers desire for us is to be holy as He is Holy. His desire for us is to have good works, to bear good fruit and to be fruitful.

In Colossians 1:9 and 10:

> *Paul prayed and said that he did not, "...cease to pray for you, and to desire that ye might be filled with the knowledge of his will in all wisdom and spiritual understanding: That ye might walk worthy of the Lord unto all pleasing, <u>being fruitful in every good work, and increasing in the knowledge of God;</u>"*

In considering this then, when in John 15:8 it says,

> *"Herein is my Father glorified, that ye bear much fruit; so shall ye be my disciples."*

and then in verse 18 when it says,

> *"Ye have not chosen me, but I have chosen you, and ordained you, that ye should go and bring*

forth fruit, and that your fruit should remain: that whatsoever ye shall ask of the Father in my name, he may give it you."

It is very clear that our Father not only wants us to bear good fruit by our good works, but that He wants us to have fruit that remains, that we live in as Christians. He wants us to, as it says in Titus 3:8 and 14, maintain good works! Line this up with Matthew 5:16 which states,

"Let your light so shine before men, that they may see your good works, and glorify your Father which is in heaven."

There can be no doubt but that we are to have good works for all to see!

We understand that we are not saved by good works, but that after we are saved are to live in good works. Ephesians 2:8-10 clearly shows us this.

"For by grace are ye saved through faith; and that not of yourselves: it is the gift of God: Not of works, lest any man should boast. For we are his workmanship, created in Christ Jesus unto good works, which God hath before ordained that we should walk in them."

This is NOT teaching as some men teach that there are ordained works that God has preordained for us to accomplish and that if we are not in the right place we cannot do the ordained works! This verse (verse 10) is simply stating that He has ordained, or that it is His will, that we **walk in good works**. We are not to sin! We are not to live in such a way that we live in bad works and have bad fruit! That is not His will! What, shall we sin? GOD FORBID!

This is one reason why so many people are skeptical of the converts of many soul winners. There is no fruit which proves their salvation and therefore they who are skeptical then criticize our soul winning and, sad to say, there is some validity to some of the criticism. No fruit! Good works, good fruit should be a natural outflow as a result of salvation!

Now, having said all of that, we must return to the fact that there are 2 kinds of fruit. There is good fruit and there is bad fruit. There are good works and there are bad works. The question in Romans 6:21 asks,

> *"What fruit had ye then in those things whereof ye are now ashamed? for the end of those things is death."*

In order to view sin as God does we must see the results of sin to help us make sin exceeding sinful and see the holiness of God and the sinfulness of man. . What are some of the results of sin? What fruit is brought forth because of sin? What happens as a result of sin? Consider the following verses.

Judges 2:15

> *"Whithersoever they went out, the hand of the LORD was against them for evil, as the LORD had said, and as the LORD had sworn unto them: and they were greatly distressed."*

Job 15:20

> *"The wicked man travaileth with pain all his days, and the number of years is hidden to the oppressor."*

Job 15:31

> *"Let not him that is deceived trust in vanity: for vanity shall be his recompence."*

Ecclesiastes 2:26

> *"For God giveth to a man that is good in his sight wisdom, and knowledge, and joy: but to the sinner he giveth travail, to gather and to heap up, that he may give to him that is good before God. This also is vanity and vexation of spirit."*

1 Chronicles 10:13 & 14

"So Saul died for his transgression which he committed against the LORD, even against the word of the LORD, which he kept not, and also for asking counsel of one that had a familiar spirit, to enquire of it;

And enquired not of the LORD: therefore he slew him, and turned the kingdom unto David the son of Jesse."

Psalm 107:17

"Fools because of their transgression, and because of their iniquities, are afflicted."

Proverbs 11:19

"As righteousness tendeth to life: so he that pursueth evil pursueth it to his own death."

Proverbs 13:15

"Good understanding giveth favour: but the way of transgressors is hard."

Romans 2:9

"Tribulation and anguish, upon every soul of man that doeth evil, of the Jew first, and also of the Gentile;"

2 Peter 2:12-19

"But these, as natural brute beasts, made to be taken and destroyed, speak evil of the things that they understand not; and shall utterly perish in their own corruption;

And shall receive the reward of unrighteousness, as they that count it pleasure to riot in the day time. Spots they are and blemishes, sporting themselves with their own deceivings while they feast with you;

Having eyes full of adultery, and that cannot cease from sin; beguiling unstable souls: an heart they have exercised with covetous practices; cursed children:

Which have forsaken the right way, and are gone astray, following the way of Balaam the son of Bosor, who loved the wages of unrighteousness;

But was rebuked for his iniquity: the dumb ass speaking with man's voice forbad the madness of the prophet.

These are wells without water, clouds that are carried with a tempest; to whom the mist of darkness is reserved for ever.

For when they speak great swelling words of vanity, they allure through the lusts of the flesh, through much wantonness, those that were clean escaped from them who live in error.

While they promise them liberty, they themselves are the servants of corruption: for of whom a man is overcome, of the same is he brought in bondage."

There are probably hundreds if not thousands more verses like these but I think you get the idea. Let me bring it home though even more. First, in Roman 6:21 it says that sin is something that we are to be ashamed of; it is something that brings death and is bad fruit. Having used this verse many times in my preaching, I ask questions like the following.

1. What good thing does drunkenness do?
2. What good thing does being high on drugs do?
3. What good thing does pornography do?
4. What good thing does adultery do?
5. What good thing does hatred do?
6. What good thing does stealing, a bad attitude, witchcraft, wrath, disobedience do?

I think you get the idea here also. The answer is always the same; there are no good things that happen in connection with sin…NOTHING GOOD!

Since we know that the fruit of sin leads to death and destruction, then it only makes sense to abstain from those things which causes so much pain and misery. This knowledge of what sin leads to should cultivate a hatred for sin and help us in our spiritual growth and understanding of how God sees sin and hopefully cause us to yield our members as members of righteousness.

In closing this chapter it is interesting to note that immediately after Romans 6:21 it says in verse 22,

> *"But now being made free from sin, and become servants to God, ye have your fruit unto holiness, and the end everlasting life."*

Then the infamous verse 23 which again sounds a clear warning in connection with a great promise,

> *"For the wages of sin is death; but the gift of God is eternal life through Jesus Christ our Lord."*

Romans 7:5

> *For when we were in the flesh, the motions of sins, which were by the law, did work in our members to bring forth fruit unto death.*

CHAPTER EIGHT

Too Late! The Damage is Done!

Numbers 32:23

"But if ye will not do so, behold, ye have sinned against the LORD: and be sure your sin will find you out."

Proverbs 6:33

"A wound and dishonour shall he get; and his reproach shall not be wiped away."

Romans 6:16

"Know ye not, that to whom ye yield yourselves servants to obey, his servants ye are to whom ye obey; whether of sin unto death, or of obedience unto righteousness?"

Romans 8:13

"For if ye live after the flesh, ye shall die: but if ye through the Spirit do mortify the deeds of the body, ye shall live."

There seems to be a mindset among today's Christians that it is no longer a big deal to sin because we can get forgiveness. They think, and it has been taught, that as long as the sin committed is not some horrible one, all the offending person needs to do is pray after the sin is committed and God will forgive them. BUT THAT IS NOT ALL THAT HAPPENS!

To fully see how truly horrible sin is we must also see what sin does; what possible consequence there are or will be. It is amazing that when we read warning signs telling of possible consequences in our national parks, most people heed the warning. Yet, when God gives us a warning, we seem to ignore it. One thing we must always remember is found in Numbers 32:23 which again states…

"But if ye will not do so, behold, ye have sinned against the LORD: and be sure your sin will find you out."

We will reap what we sow!

Galatians 6:7 - 8

"Be not deceived; God is not mocked: for whatsoever a man soweth, that shall he also reap. For he that soweth to his flesh shall of the flesh reap corruption; but he that soweth to the Spirit shall of the Spirit reap life everlasting."

In one of the sources I have on my laptop it says,

"The idea that men may be selfish and continue in sin, and yet escape punishment is vain..."

Another wrote,

"...the heart of man seems to be chiefly overpowered and prevailed upon by two motives for sin, first, the SECRECY in committing sin, and secondly, IMPUNITY WITH RESPECT TO ITS CONSEQUENCES!"

Both of these motives are false! They think that God does not see our sin which is not true at all. He does! But the one I want to concentrate on in this chapter is the thought that we can sin and somehow avoid the consequences. As the quote mentioned, we think we can sin because we have, "impunity with respect to its consequences."

I just looked up "impunity" and it means, "Exemption from punishment or penalty." It also correctly states, "Impunity encourages men in crimes." This also agrees with Ecclesiastes 8:11 which says,

"Because sentence against an evil work is not executed speedily, therefore the heart of the sons of men is fully set in them to do evil."

We normally stop with that verse but look at what verses 12 and 13 teach us.

"Though a sinner do evil an hundred times, and his days be prolonged, yet surely I know that it shall be well with them that fear God, which fear before him: But it shall not be well with the wicked, neither shall he prolong his days, which are as a shadow; because he feareth not before God."

We must understand and remember that when we sin, there are two things that happen. **First, damage has been done and second, that there are always consequences.**

In studying and gathering information for this book I found the following statement which, I believe, is an accurate one. **"Most Christians rarely, if ever, ask God for forgiveness when they sin."** There seems to be no remorse for the sin that is committed, which stems from the line of thinking today that repenting does not include a change of mind about sin, but only a change of mind about belief. More will be said about this in another chapter but there needs to be some level of sadness, remorse, and or conviction about having sinned against our loving, longsuffering heavenly Father. I am not saying that there needs to be copious tears every time we sin, but, then again....WHY NOT! Have we "advanced" so much in Christianity that we shed no tears? Are we so right with God that there is no remorse for sin? I think not. Would to God we had tears again for sin and for sinners. Could we have such a revival by the Holy Spirit that we actually wept over our sin and over sinfulness that in all of it He is glorified? Can there actually be anyone who would disagree with this? Oh, that we would so cultivate a relationship with our Father, and so want to please Him and be very sensitive to the Holy Spirit that we would rush to the throne of Grace to confess and forsake our sin AND at the same time abhor what we did!

A friend of mind Dr. Lance Ketchum wrote,

"I have never known repentance to come from anything else that a genuine understanding of God's hatred for sin and His consequential, imminent and pending judgment upon all sin and sinners. Genuine repentance is birthed from understanding God's hatred of thought sins (lust), heart sins (out of control emotions), and walk sins (sinful acts of moral turpitude)."

If we would also come to understand that the moment we sin, there is damage that has been done that cannot be undone, it might cause us to stop and consider what we are thinking about doing and cause us to fall on our face before a Holy and Just God! Though it is not too late to ask forgiveness when we sin, it is too late to undo the damage.

In Romans 8:6 and 13 it says,

"For to be carnally minded is death; but to be spiritually minded is life and peace."

"For if ye live after the flesh, ye shall die: but if ye through the Spirit do mortify the deeds of the body, ye shall live."

Look at the results of being carnally minded.....death! Look at the results of being of the flesh....death! Most diseases do not kill us immediately but most diseases are a result of something in the body which should not be there. Many times we ingest, inhale, and drink things into our body which were never intended to be in there. You can stop (repent) doing whatever is was that you were doing to your body, but the damage has been done! This is not a popular thought, but the Bible still says,

"Wherefore, as by one man sin entered into the world, and death by sin; and so death passed upon all men, for that all have sinned:"

Take a look at these verses thinking about what irreversible damage is done because of sin.

Psalm 38:4

"For mine iniquities are gone over mine head: as an heavy burden they are too heavy for me."

Psalm 38:5

"My wounds stink and are corrupt because of my foolishness."

Psalm 51:3

"For I acknowledge my transgressions: and my sin is ever before me."

Proverbs 6:26-35

"For by means of a whorish woman a man is brought to a piece of bread: and the adulteress will hunt for the precious life. Can a man take fire in his bosom, and his clothes not be burned? Can one go upon hot coals, and his feet not be burned? So he that goeth in to his neighbour's wife; whosoever toucheth her shall not be innocent. Men do not despise a thief, if he steal to satisfy his soul when he is hungry; But if he be found, he shall restore sevenfold; he shall give all the substance of his house. But whoso committeth adultery with a woman lacketh understanding: he that doeth it destroyeth his own soul. A wound and dishonour shall he get; and his reproach shall not be wiped away. For jealousy is the rage of a man: therefore he will not spare in the day of vengeance. He will not regard any ransom; neither will he rest content, though thou givest many gifts."

Proverbs 23:29-35

"Who hath woe? who hath sorrow? who hath contentions? who hath babbling? who hath wounds without cause? who hath redness of eyes? They that tarry long at the wine; they that go to seek mixed wine. Look not thou upon the wine when it is red, when it giveth his colour in the cup, when it moveth itself aright. At the last it biteth like a serpent, and stingeth like an adder. Thine eyes shall behold strange women, and thine heart shall utter perverse things. Yea, thou shalt be as he that lieth down in the midst of the sea, or as he that lieth upon the top of a mast.

They have stricken me, shalt thou say, and I was not sick; they have beaten me, and I felt it not: when shall I awake? I will seek it yet again."

Damage is done whenever we sin, and it is irreversible. I found this as I was studying and researching for this material. "It is better to stay pure than to try to regain what was lost and cannot be found." Once the damage has been inflicted, it is done!

When you lie, the damage is done. When you gossip, damage is done. When you cheat, the damage is done. When you stay out of church, damage is done. When you neglect your spouse, there is damage that is done.

Will we sin? Yes! Can we be forgiven? Yes! Should we sin? No! But when we do din there is some level of damage has been inflicted. It may be physical, mental, financial, damage to a reputation, spiritual damage, damage to a relationship or damage to character, but there is damage. Damage that is irreversible, or possibly damage that will take some time to get past, but damage none the less.

David caused a lot of damage in his adulterous relationship with Bathsheba. Judas Iscariots suicide was irreversible. The damage Saul inflicted because of his disobedience was irreversible. Achan's rebellion caused damage to the nation Israel and eventually his own family and when they died because of his sin, it was irreversible. Even if the penalty is not death, there is damage done because of sin. Always remember, sin when it is finished bringeth forth death, there is always a consequence for sin. We must recognize that when we sin, it is too late to stop the damage, the damage is done!

CHAPTER NINE

The Effect of Sin on You and Others

Numbers 14:26-37

"And the LORD spake unto Moses and unto Aaron, saying, How long shall I bear with this evil congregation, which murmur against me? I have heard the murmurings of the children of Israel, which they murmur against me. Say unto them, As truly as I live, saith the LORD, as ye have spoken in mine ears, so will I do to you: Your carcases shall fall in this wilderness; and all that were numbered of you, according to your whole number, from twenty years old and upward, which have murmured against me, Doubtless ye shall not come into the land, concerning which I sware to make you dwell therein, save Caleb the son of Jephunneh, and Joshua the son of Nun. But your little ones, which ye said should be a prey, them will I bring in, and they shall know the land which ye have despised. But as for you, your carcases, they shall fall in this wilderness. And your children shall wander in the wilderness forty years, and bear your whoredoms, until your carcases be wasted in the wilderness. After the number of the days in which ye searched the land, even forty days, each day for a year, shall ye bear your iniquities, even forty years, and ye shall know my breach of promise. I the LORD have said, I will surely do it unto all this evil congregation, that are gathered together against me: in this wilderness they shall be consumed, and there they shall die. And the men, which Moses sent to search the land, who returned, and made all the congregation to murmur against him, by bringing up a slander upon the land, Even those men that did bring up the evil report upon the land, died by the plague before the LORD."

Psalm 37:28

"For the LORD loveth judgment, and forsaketh not his saints; they are preserved for ever: but the seed of the wicked shall be cut off."

1 Peter 2:6-10

"Wherefore also it is contained in the scripture, Behold, I lay in Sion a chief corner stone, elect, precious: and he that believeth on him shall not be confounded. Unto you therefore which believe he is precious: but unto them which be disobedient, the stone which the builders disallowed, the same is made the head of the corner, And a stone of stumbling, and a rock of offence, even to them which stumble at the word, being disobedient: whereunto also they were appointed. But ye are a chosen generation, a royal priesthood, an holy nation, a peculiar people; that ye should shew forth the praises of him who hath called you out of darkness into his marvellous light: Which in time past were not a people, but are now the people of God: which had not obtained mercy, but now have obtained mercy."

It should go without saying that what we do and what we do not do affects others. If we do good, it is not only good for us but also good for others. If we do evil, it not only hurts us but it also hurts others. This should be a motivating thought that causes us to seriously consider what we do.

Matthew 5:16 shows us that our right living is seen by others and it also glorifies our Father in heaven.

"Let your light so shine before men, that they may see your good works, and glorify your Father which is in heaven."

In 1 Corinthians 8:3 it states,

"But if any man love God, the same is known of him."

Clearly, how we act, what we do, where we go and what we say affects others. This is especially true when we sin! Our sinfulness affecting others is also clearly stated in Romans 5:12 and 19 which say,

Romans 5:12

"Wherefore, as by one man sin entered into the world, and death by sin; and so death passed upon all men, for that all have sinned:"

Romans 5:19

"For as by one man's disobedience many were made sinners, so by the obedience of one shall many be made righteous."

What Adam and Eve did has affected all of mankind since the Garden of Eden! Sin always affects others! What about when you and I sin? How does it affect others? How will it affect my family, my future and my country? We see clear examples of this in the lives of Lot, King Saul, King David, Achan and in the history of the nation Israel itself. Sin always has consequences and sin always affects others! ALWAYS!

May I remind you that sin is the breaking of the law or commands of God and there are always consequences and heart ache! When Achan sinned by not obeying the simple commands that were given to the whole nation, not only did he not enjoy the sin but eventually his family died and others died also! Sin always affects others! His sin not only affected him personally but, as I said, others in the nation actually died because of his sin! It affected their relationship with God and it affected his own ability to glorify God! Sin always has consequences and affects others! He lost his possessions, his life, his eternal reputation, and his family who were stoned and all their possessions burned. Your sin not only affects you but it also affects others! And, as I stated in another chapter, when we sin, damage is always done!

We know the story of Lot, how he looked toward the well-watered plains of Jordan choosing to take his herds there so they could separate from Abraham and his herds. I guess I really do not blame him for looking that way. He made a business decision based on what was best for his herds. He had a lot of livestock and water is a rare commodity in much of Israel. He was only interested in making sure his herds were well watered and fed. I am sure if he had known what was to follow, he would not have gone that way, what loving and responsible husband and father would? But, next, we see him sitting in the gate with the men of the city and the Scripture says in 2 Peter 2:8,

> *"(For that righteous man dwelling among them, in seeing and hearing, vexed his righteous soul from day to day with their unlawful deeds;)"*

Lot, because of his location, vexed his righteous soul by constantly seeing and hearing all the wickedness of the city. The sins of the city affected him so much that he eventually offered his daughters to the wicked men of Sodom. But that is not all, the sin also affected his sons in law, his daughters who were married to them and eventually lost his wife in death not to mention all their worldly possessions. He even committed incest with his daughters after they got him drunk and the children from that illegitimate relationship affect people even today. BE SURE YOUR SIN WILL FIND YOU OUT! AND IT WILL AFFECT OTHERS.

In the verses called the Ten Commandments is this warning from God.

Exodus 20:3-6

> *"Thou shalt have no other gods before me. Thou shalt not make unto thee any graven image, or any likeness of any thing that is in heaven above, or that is in the earth beneath, or that is in the water under the earth: Thou shalt not bow down thyself to them, nor serve them: for I the LORD thy God am a jealous God, <u>visiting the iniquity of the fathers upon the children unto the third and fourth</u>*

generation of them that hate me; And shewing mercy unto thousands of them that love me, and keep my commandments."

In his commentary on the Bible the well-known Baptist John Gill writes on verse 5,

"Thou shall not bow down thyself to them,.... Perform any worship to them, show any reverence of them by any gesture of the body; one being mentioned, bowing the body, and put for all others, as prostration of it to the earth, bending the knee, kissing the hand, lifting up of hands or eyes to them, or by any outward action expressing a religious esteem of them, as if there was divinity in them:

nor serve them; in a religious manner, internally or externally, by offering sacrifice and burning incense to them; by praying to, or praising of them; by expressing love to them, faith and trust in them, hope and expectation of good things from them, and the like. The reason of this second command, relating to the making and worshipping of images, next follows:

for I the Lord thy God am a jealous God; jealous of his own honour and glory, and will not give it to another; even to graven images, nor suffer it to be given to them without resenting it; and jealousy is fierce and cruel, and breaks forth into great wrath, and issues in dreadful scenes oftentimes among men; as a man that has reason to be jealous of his wife, and especially if he takes her and the adulterer in the fact, it often costs them both their lives, being so enraged at such an insult upon him, and such a violation of the marriage bed; and thus the great Jehovah, the God of Israel, their head and husband, is represented, in order to deter from idolatry, or spiritual adultery, than which nothing could be more provoking to him:

visiting the iniquity of the fathers upon the children; meaning chiefly, if not solely, the iniquity of idolatry; which being such an insult on his honour, "crimen laesae majestatis", is treated by him as high treason is among men; not only he punishes the authors and perpetrators of it in their own persons, which is meant by "visiting", but upon their children also, which are parts of themselves; and whatsoever is inflicted on them is the same as on themselves, and is an addition to, and a sensible aggravation of their punishment; and especially these are visited in such a manner, when they tread in their father's steps, and fill up the measure of their iniquity. So the Targum of Jonathan,"visiting the iniquity of ungodly fathers on rebellious children:

unto the third and fourth generation of them that hate me; as all idolaters must be thought to do, whatsoever love and affection they may pretend to God, by worshipping idols before him, besides him, along with him, or him in them: "the third and fourth generation" are mentioned, because sometimes parents lived to see these, and so with their eyes beheld the punishment inflicted upon their posterity for their sins, which must be distressing to them; or, however, these being but small removes from them, might impress their minds and affect them, to think what their sins would bring upon their descendants, who would quickly come after them, and share in the sad effects of their iniquities, and so be a means to deter them from them."

Surely this ought to be a resounding warning to all of us that what we do affects others not only by some sort of punishment as in the case of Achan and Lot, but what we do sets an example and our children will do the same things. Our sin affects others!

Sin is such a life destroying thing not only for the one committing the sin, but for those who are affected by it. Recently the sin of one man has affected the lives of thousands and even the ability of Independent Baptist churches to reach more people for Christ. The sins of another man have affected countless people who looked up to him but because of his adulterous life he is now not trusted by many. Sin is so, so devastating! Sin when it is finished surely brings forth death! The wages of sin is death! Death passed upon all men for that all have sinned! Oh how awful sin is!

Your sin may not seem like much to you now, but it will and it may not seem like such a big deal....BUT IT IS. There is no such thing as a small sin! All sin is death dealing. All sin is vile to God and all sin affects others! Do you really want to pay the price and do you really want others to do likewise because of your sin?

Above all others there is an effect of our sin on God! Just imagine what God's heart must feel when we sin! He loves righteousness and hates iniquity as found in Hebrews 1:9. YES, SIN IS AN ABOMINATION WITH GOD AND IF OUR RIGHTEOSNESSES LOOK FILTHY, WHAT DO OUR SINS LOOK LIKE? Sin not only is seen in His eyes as something worse than filthy rags, but sin causes Him to turn His Holy eyes away from us as it did while His Son Jesus was paying for the sins of all mankind on the cross. (1 Peter 2:24) A very important part of that verse says, "...that we, being dead to sins, should live unto righteousness..." We are to no longer live in sin! (Romans 6:2)

Oh! But when we do sin we so break the heart of our Father! It ought to break our heart when we sin and say like David when he was confronted with his sin with Bathsheba, "I HAVE SINNED!"

When we sin we cause Him to turn from us so that He will not hear our prayers. (Psalm 66:18) Oh, the awful affects not only on us but on others of that vile thing called sin! How the Father must grieve over our sinfulness, but thanks be to God for His Son Jesus Who gives us the victory through His sacrificial death. But our sins even affected the Son of God and can grieve the Holy Spirit in us.

No wonder Paul wrote, "O wretched man that I am…" Our sinfulness always has a negative affect and it affects others.

CHAPTER TEN

Whose Servant Are You?

Romans 6:1-23

"What shall we say then? Shall we continue in sin, that grace may abound? God forbid. How shall we, that are dead to sin, live any longer therein? Know ye not, that so many of us as were baptized into Jesus Christ were baptized into his death? Therefore we are buried with him by baptism into death: that like as Christ was raised up from the dead by the glory of the Father, even so we also should walk in newness of life. For if we have been planted together in the likeness of his death, we shall be also in the likeness of his resurrection: Knowing this, that our old man is crucified with him, that the body of sin might be destroyed, that henceforth we should not serve sin. For he that is dead is freed from sin. Now if we be dead with Christ, we believe that we shall also live with him: Knowing that Christ being raised from the dead dieth no more; death hath no more dominion over him. For in that he died, he died unto sin once: but in that he liveth, he liveth unto God. Likewise reckon ye also yourselves to be dead indeed unto sin, but alive unto God through Jesus Christ our Lord. Let not sin therefore reign in your mortal body, that ye should obey it in the lusts thereof. Neither yield ye your members as instruments of unrighteousness unto sin: but yield yourselves unto God, as those that are alive from the dead, and your members as instruments of righteousness unto God. For sin shall not have dominion over you: for ye are not under the law, but under grace. What then? shall we sin, because we are not under the law, but under grace? God forbid. Know ye not, that to whom ye yield yourselves servants to obey, his servants ye are to whom ye obey; whether of sin unto death,

or of obedience unto righteousness? But God be thanked, that ye (were the servants of sin, but ye have obeyed from the heart that form of doctrine which was delivered you. Being then made free from sin, ye became the servants of righteousness. I speak after the manner of men because of the infirmity of your flesh: for as ye have yielded your members servants to uncleanness and to iniquity unto iniquity; even so now yield your members servants to righteousness unto holiness. For when ye were the servants of sin, ye were free from righteousness. What fruit had ye then in those things whereof ye are now ashamed? for the end of those things is death. But now being made free from sin, and become servants to God, ye have your fruit unto holiness, and the end everlasting life. For the wages of sin is death; but the gift of God is eternal life through Jesus Christ our Lord."

A friend of mine, Dr. Lance Ketchum, recently posted this on the internet,

"Those that teach that repentance is just a change of mind often leave out that the change of mind involves the want to abandon the corruption of sin as well."

A close look at Romans 6 will back up that statement one-hundred percent. There is something that happens at salvation that even our baptism shows. I will say more about repentance and baptism later but in order to write on the title of this chapter, I also wanted to lay some general ground work first.

One of the statements we have heard expressed, and have said myself, is that if there is no conviction, there is no conversion. (I also found that statement in a book by A. W. Tozer but am not sure that he is the one who said it originally.) But, I have to ask a question, conviction of what? The answer is simple, conviction of sin! If sin has nothing to do with us before salvation as I have heard, then why do we use the Roman Road to witness to people where the very first point we make is that the person is a sinner? We point to verses like Roman 3:10 and 23 because we are sinners but if sin has nothing to do with salvation then, again, why do we start out pointing out that people are sinners? The reason we are lost is because we are sinners and the Holy Spirit "reproves the world of sin!" (John 16:8) Sin is a part of our leading a person to Christ and must be dealt with!

When Jesus was speaking to the people one day, He said in John 8:31-34,

> *"Then said Jesus to those Jews which believed on him, If ye continue in my word, then are ye my disciples indeed; And ye shall know the truth, and the truth shall make you free. They answered him, We be Abraham's seed, and were never in bondage to any man: how sayest thou, Ye shall be made free? Jesus answered them, Verily, verily, I say unto you, Whosoever committeth sin is the servant of sin."*

A very important point of that set of verses is found in verse 34 which states,

> *"...Verily, verily, I say unto you, Whosoever committeth sin is the servant of sin."*

In his comments on this verse John Gill wrote,

> "...this is to be understood of such whose bias and bent of their minds are to sin; who give up themselves unto it, and sell themselves to work wickedness; who make sin their trade, business, and employment, and are properly workers of it, and take delight and pleasure in it: these, whatever liberty, they promise themselves, are the servants of corruption; they are under the government of sin, that has dominion over them; and they obey it in the lusts thereof, and are drudges and slaves unto it, and will have no other wages at last but death, even eternal death, if grace prevent not;"

The point of Romans chapter six is that before salvation, we were servants to sin. Now that we are saved, which is an interesting word to be mentioned again later, we are NOT the servants of sin, or we should not be. There is a difference in our direction and this difference takes place at the time of our salvation because of conviction of sin and repentance.

The conviction of sin is a part of what leads us to our decision to trust in Christ. A recognition of our sinfulness in the sight of a Holy God Who sent His Son to die for our sins (John 3:16), leads us to our decision to believe or trust in that Christ Who died on the cross to pay for our sins. (See Romans 3:23)

Basically, at salvation we not only trust in Christ for our salvation, but there is also at least some level of change of attitude about sin which leads to a change of direction. It is NOT a repenting of all sin in order to get saved; it is an acceptance of the fact of sin and our sinfulness. After salvation begins the realization that we were the servants of sin but are now to live in obedience to God's will and we are not to live in sin anymore! God forbid! How shall we that are dead to sin live any longer therein? We should not and it starts at salvation.

There are two very important questions at the beginning of Romans chapter six. The first one is, "Shall we CONTINUE in sin, that grace may abound?" The answer of course to this is GOD FORBID! But, before we get to the next question, look at the word, "continue." It comes from the Greek word, "epimeno" and means, "to stay over, remain, abide, continue and tarry." The question is, should we remain, stay over or continue in sin after we get saved? Again, emphatically, NO! GOD FORBIDS IT! We are not to stay in sin. Why? The question, "How shall we that are DEAD TO SIN, LIVE ANY LONGER THEREIN?" (Romans 6:2) When did we die to sin? Romans 6:6 gives us an insight into the answer.

> *"Knowing this, that <u>our old man is crucified with him</u>, that the body of sin might be destroyed, that <u>henceforth we should not serve sin.</u>"*

Our OLD MAN, the man of sin before salvation, our non-born again man is crucified with Him. When does this happen? When we come to the cross for salvation! We are crucified with Him, why? THAT THE BODY OF SIN MIGHT BE DESTROYED **THAT WE SHOULD NOT SERVE SIN** (like we used to). WE ARE NO LONGER LIKE WE USED TO BE! WE ARE NO LONGER TO BE THE SERVANTS OF SIN! WHY? Because we have seen ourselves through the eyes of God as the sinners that we are, we see our need of the Saviour Who died on the cross and we then trust Him as our Saviour and the things we used to do we disdain to do them anymore. The body of sin is crucified with Him and we are to rise up to walk in the newness of life!

Romans 6:2b-7

"...How shall we, that are dead to sin, live any longer therein?

Know ye not, that so many of us as were baptized into Jesus Christ were baptized into his death?

Therefore we are buried with him by baptism into death: that like as Christ was raised up from the dead by the glory of the Father, even so we also should walk in newness of life. For if we have been planted together in the likeness of his death, we shall be also in the likeness of his resurrection:

Knowing this, that our old man is crucified with him, that the body of sin might be destroyed, that henceforth we should not serve sin.

For he that is dead is freed from sin.

I heartily believe that there is to begin to be a difference about sin in a person's life when they get saved because of their decision to get saved.

I will probably put this quote from Spurgeon in the chapter on repentance but I want to also put it here. It sounds like it could have been written today.

"True repentance is always accompanied by sorrow. It has been said by some of those of modern times who disparage repentance that repentance is "nothing but a change of mind." These words sound as if there was merely some superficial meaning to them; and so, indeed, that are intended by those who use them, but they are not so intended by the Spirit of God. Repentance may be and is a change of mind; but what a change it is! It is not an unimportant change of mind such as you may have concerning whether you will take you holiday this week or the next, or about some trifling matter of domestic interest; but it is a change of mind of the whole heart, of the love, of the hate, of the judgment, and their view of things taken by the individual whose mind is thus changed. It is a deep, radical, fundamental, lasting change; and you will find that, whenever you meet with it in Scripture, it is always accompanied with sorrow for past sin. And rest you assured of this fact, that the repentance which has no tear in its eye, and no mourning for sin in its heart, is a repentance which needs to be repented of, for there is no evidence of conversion, no sign of the existence of the grace of God. In what way has that man changed his mind who is not sorry that he has sinned? In what sense can it be said the he has undergone any change worth experiencing if he can look back upon his past life with pleasure, or look upon the prospect of returning to his sin without an inward loathing and disgust.

I say again that we have need to stand in doubt of that repentance which is not accompanied with mourning for sin; and even when Christ is clearly seen by faith, and sin is pardoned, and the man knows that it is forgiven, he does not cease to mourn for sin. Nay, brethren, his mourning becomes deeper as his knowledge of his guilt increases; and his hatred of sin grows in proportion as he understands that love of Christ by which his sin is put away!"

Can anyone in anyway refute this? Is there anyone who can truly say that he was wrong? I imagine that there are some who would take this to task, but then read Romans 6 again! Take that to task!

Whose servant are you? Whose servant should you be as a Christian? In my Bible above chapter 8 which continues the discussion about sin, I have printed, "God's Health Program" with verses 12 and 13 and I Timothy 4:8 referred to. These verses say,

Romans 8:12 & 13

"Therefore, brethren, we are debtors, not to the flesh, to live after the flesh. For if ye live after the flesh, ye shall die: but if ye through the Spirit do mortify the deeds of the body, ye shall live."

1 Timothy 4:8

"For bodily exercise profiteth little: but godliness is profitable unto all things, having promise of the life that now is, and of that which is to come."

These verses and many others tell us how to live longer. How do we live longer? Romans 6:16 answers this.

"Know ye not, that to whom ye yield yourselves servants to obey, his servants ye are to whom ye obey; whether of sin unto death, or of obedience unto righteousness?"

Whose servant are you and what is the benefit connected with that master? If you are the servant of righteousness doing the best you can to live righteously as a Christian, then it is life. On the other hand, if you are a servant of wickedness then your reward is death. As people like to say today, "That is a no brainer!"

When we yield ourselves as a servant of sin, it leads to death. Sin always leads to death! Sin when it is finished bringeth forth death! The wages of sin is death! The soul that sinneth shall die! As by one man sin entered into the world and death by sin, therefore sin passed upon all men!

Alcohol leads to death! Immorality leads to death! When David had an adulterous affair with Bathsheba, it lead to death! Drugs lead to death. I could go on and on and on. Whose servant are you?

But, at salvation we chose Christ for salvation in effect recognizing our sins and became the servants of righteousness. God's health program is to live a Godly life, not a sinful one and remember, we have been crucified with Christ!

We as Christians have a choice to make and then continue making that decision. That choice is to live and have fruit of the Spirit and not the fruit of the flesh.

Another interesting question that is asked is found in Romans 6:21 which reads,

> *"What fruit had ye then in those things whereof ye are now ashamed? for the end of those things is death."*

An easy way to figure out whose servant you are; look at the fruit or the results of your actions. When John the Baptist said, "Bring forth fruits meet (suitable, or in agreement with) for repentance," then we too should have fruit or results that are meet or compatible with repentance! We should be servants of righteousness not the servants of sin! Our old man has been crucified with Him...that we should not serve sin. (Verse 6). We are dead to sin (verse 11), we are not to let sin reign in our mortal body to obey it BECAUSE WE ARE NOT THE SERVANTS OF SIN! (Verse 12) We are not to yield our members to unrighteousness and sin, but are to yield to God and our members to Him! (Verse 14) Sin is not to have dominion over us (verse 14) and we ARE (present tense) the servant of righteousness by our faith in Christ! (Verse 18)

Though we use the following verse to witness to the lost, this verse is a warning to Christians.

Romans 6:23

*"For the wages of sin is death; but the gift of God
is eternal life through Jesus Christ our Lord."*

Whose Servant are YOU?

CHAPTER ELEVEN

Repent!

William Booth said,

> "The chief danger of the twentieth century will be: religion without the Holy Ghost, Christianity without Christ, forgiveness without repentance, salvation without regeneration, heaven without hell."

There have always been those dangers and they have been prevalent many times throughout history.

Repentance now days is one of those subjects which will cause good men to part company, argue and even get into name calling. It is always amazing to me how one side will always call the other side "liberal" if they do not agree with them. Whenever that happens, I always look closely to the side accusing the other side to be liberal with suspicion. It seems the ones who are always wrong are the name callers. Well, enough on that.

Why is this division and name calling happening? Because of the watering down of what repentance is and is not. I believe that, just like sin, repentance has been watered and dumbed down to the point where either one is very, very weak. The reason it has been watered down is because it is not in our "comfort zone." Sin and repentance are not pleasant to talk about or accurately define. Our political correctness era makes Biblical preaching about these subjects uncomfortable and offensive. We have taken the sting out of sin and repentance. We have taken the remorse out of repentance and given it a very touchy-feely definition. They are saying, "We don't need to worry about sin, because it is really no big deal." They have said that repentance is only going from unbelief to belief and has nothing to do with sin before salvation! Spurgeon had that to deal with too in his day. I know I put this quote in earlier but I wanted to re-emphasize it in this book so here it is again.

"True repentance is always accompanied by sorrow. <u>It has been said by some of those of modern times who disparage repentance that repentance is "nothing but a change of mind."</u> These words sound as if there was merely some superficial meaning to them; and so, indeed, that are intended by those who use them, but they are not so intended by the Spirit of God. Repentance may be and is a change of mind; but what a change it is! It is not an unimportant change of mind such as you may have concerning whether you will take you holiday this week or the next, or about some trifling matter of domestic interest; but it is a change of mind of the whole heart, of the love, of the hate, of the judgment, and their view of things taken by the individual whose mind is thus changed. It is a deep, radical, fundamental, lasting change; and you will find that, whenever you meet with it in Scripture, it is always accompanied with sorrow for past sin. And rest you assured of this fact, that the repentance which has no tear in its eye, and no mourning for sin in its heart, is a repentance which needs to be repented of, for there is no evidence of conversion, no sign of the existence of the grace of God. In what way has that man changed his mind who is not sorry that he has sinned? In what sense can it be said the he has undergone any change worth experiencing if he can look back upon his past life with pleasure, or look upon the prospect of returning to his sin without an inward loathing and disgust.

I say again that we have need to stand in doubt of that repentance which is not accompanied with mourning for sin; and even when Christ is clearly seen by faith, and sin is pardoned, and the man knows that it is forgiven, he does not cease to mourn for sin. Nay, brethren, his mourning becomes deeper as his knowledge of his guilt increases; and his hatred of sin grows in proportion as he understands that love of Christ by which his sin is put away!"

What? Sin is no big deal? You do not have to repent of sin? I beg to differ with you and that line of thought, and I will do it

Scripturally and historically to prove that that line of teaching is not only wrong but heretical.

Before I go any further, let me tell you what I believe. No! You do not need to repent of all your sins in order to get saved. I am not a Lordship salvation person, but, yes, we should repent (have a change of mind) of sin (singular), which will then lead us to the Saviour for salvation. I recognize sin as being hateful towards God, I see sin and I am a sinner who needs a Saviour. I am convinced of sin and turn to Christ for salvation and also have a new desire to live for Him and to abstain from sin. All of that taking place at salvation. Repentance for sin does come before and after salvation. When we see ourselves as a sinner and have need of a Saviour, we have a level of remorse which leads us to faith in Christ. It leads us to an acceptance of Christ because we see that our sins have come between us and God and we deserve the wages of sin which is death and hell.

If repentance of sin has nothing to do with salvation, then why do we tell people they are sinners? Why, as we witness to people do we use Romans 3:10 and 23? Why do we tell people Romans 6:23 if repentance, or a change of mind about sin, has nothing to do with salvation? Why do we say no conviction no conversion if repentance of sin has nothing to do with salvation? And, may I say, conviction does no simply mean we admit we are sinners. I read once that even a wicked man will admit he is a sinner, but then have no change in his behavior. He will admit his sinfulness and have no repentance in his heart for it. If as we witness to people we lead them in a sinner's prayer and start out with, "I know I am a sinner, forgive me of my sin..." then repentance of sin must be a part of salvation! Why do we tell people they need a Saviour that they need to trust Christ as the Saviour Who has paid for all our sins if repentance of sin has nothing to do with salvation? Yes! Emphatically, yes! Repentance of sin is a part of salvation. A change of mind about sin happens leading us into our salvation. When I was under conviction for my sinfulness, it led me to my faith in Christ to save me from sins penalty and to give me eternal life.

Sin is exceeding sinful and must be repented of if a person is to truly come to Christ. If we are commanded to TURN FROM sin to re-establish a good relationship with God AFTER salvation, then why, according to some, don't we have to also repent of sin in order to come to Him for salvation?

Jonah, when he finally got to Nineveh said,

"... Yet forty days, and Nineveh shall be overthrown." (Jonah 3:4b)

What was the response of the people from the King down that got God's attention, which also caused Him to not destroy them?

Jonah 3:5-10

"So the people of Nineveh believed God, and proclaimed a fast, and put on sackcloth, from the greatest of them even to the least of them. For word came unto the king of Nineveh, and he arose from his throne, and he laid his robe from him, and covered him with sackcloth, and sat in ashes. And he caused it to be proclaimed and published through Nineveh by the decree of the king and his nobles, saying, Let neither man nor beast, herd nor flock, taste any thing: let them not feed, nor drink water: But let man and beast be covered with sackcloth, and cry mightily unto God: yea, let them turn every one from his evil way, and from the violence that is in their hands. Who can tell if God will turn and repent, and turn away from his fierce anger, that we perish not? And God saw their works, that they turned from their evil way; and God repented of the evil, that he had said that he would do unto them; and he did it not."

According to some the narrative should have just ended at, "So the people believed God..." at verse 5, since repentance is only going from unbelief to belief. But, it is more than that. It is

REPENTANCE and FAITH! The people were sinners because of their evil ways and their violence. The preaching of Jonah pointed that out and the people were not right with God. They believed the preaching and it brought conviction of sin!

The people of Nineveh acknowledged their sinfulness by the sackcloth and ashes. Understanding their need to turn from their evil ways and their violence, THEN God saw they were serious and He repented, or changed His mind, about destroying them and He did not.

Now some object to this saying that the people were trying to get right with God by their works, or, a works salvation. This is not what they were attempting to do. They saw their sinfulness in light of what God said and turned from it. They were repenting of their sinfulness! They were turning from their sinfulness toward God for their salvation! When a person hears the Gospel which includes the fact of our sinfulness and the Holiness of God, and He believes the message and by faith repents and trusts the Son of God for their salvation, God then sees our heart and saves us from the penalty of sin and gives us eternal life. Not because we give up all our sins, but because we see our sins, our need of a Saviour, and that Jesus is the Christ Who died for the penalty of sin. It all has to do with sin!

Don't tell me that repentance of sin has nothing to do with salvation! That is what leads to it!

Second Corinthians 7:10 says,

"For godly sorrow worketh repentance to salvation not to be repented of: but the sorrow of the world worketh death."

From Adam Clarke's Commentary on the whole Bible on this verse he wrote,

"For godly sorrow - That which has the breach of God's holy law for its object.

Worketh repentance - A thorough change of mind unto salvation, because the person who feels it cannot rest till he finds pardon through the mercy of God.

But the sorrow of the world worketh death - Sorrow for lost goods, lost friends, death of relatives, etc., when it is poignant and deep, produces diseases, increases those that already exist, and often leads men to lay desperate hands on themselves. This sorrow leads to destruction, the other leads to salvation; the one leads to heaven, the other to hell."

In the Geneva Bible notes is this,

"God's sorrow occurs when we are not terrified with the fear of punishment, but because we feel we have offended God our most merciful Father. Contrary to this there is another sorrow, that only fears punishment, or when a man is vexed for the loss of some worldly goods. The fruit of the first is repentance, and the fruit of the second is desperation, unless the Lord quickly helps."

In Albert Barnes Notes on the New Testament it says,

"Verse 10. <u>For godly sorrow.</u> "Sorrow according, to God," That is, such sorrow as has respect to God, or is according to his will, or as leads the soul to him. This is a very important expression in regard to true repentance, and shows the exact nature of that sorrow which is connected with a return to God. The phrase may be regarded as implying the following things:

(1.) Such sorrow as God approves, or such as is suitable to, or conformable to his will and desires., It cannot mean that it is such sorrow or grief as God has, for he has none; but such as shall be in accordance with what God demands in a return to him. It is a sorrow which his truth is fitted to produce on the heart; such a sorrow as shall appropriately arise from viewing sin as God views it; such sorrow as exists in the mind when our views accord with his in regard to the existence, the extent, the nature, and the ill-desert of sin. Such views will lead to sorrow that it has ever been committed; and such views will be "according to God."

(2.) Such sorrow as shall be exercised towards God in view of sin; which shall arise from a view of the evil of sin as committed against a holy God. It is not mainly that it will lead to pain; that it will overwhelm the soul in disgrace; that it will forfeit the favour or lead to the contempt of man; or that it will lead to an eternal hell; but, it is such as arises from a view of the evil of sin as committed against a holy and just God. It is not mainly from the fact that it is an offence against his infinite majesty. Such sorrow David had (Ps 51:4) when he said, "Against thee, thee only have I sinned;" when the offence regarded as committed against man, enormous as it was, was lost and absorbed in its greater evil when regarded as committed against God. So all true and genuine repentance is that which regards sin as deriving its main evil from the fact that it is committed against God.

(3.) That which leads to God. It leads to God to obtain forgiveness --to seek for consolation. A heart truly contrite and penitent seeks God, and implores pardon from him. Other sorrow in view of sin than that which is genuine repentance, leads the person away from God. He seeks consolation in the world; he endeavours to drive away his serious impressions, or to drown them in the pleasures and the cares of life. But genuine sorrow for sin leads the soul to God, and conducts the sinner, through the Redeemer, to him to obtain the pardon and peace which he only can give to a wounded spirit. In God alone can pardon and true peace be found; and godly sorrow for sin will seek them there.

Worketh repentance. Produces a change that shall be permanent; a reformation. It is not mere regret; it does not soon pass away in its effects, but it produces permanent and abiding changes. A man who mourns over sin as committed against God, and who seeks to God for pardon, will reform his life, and truly repent. He who has grief for sin only because it will lead to disgrace or shame, or because it will lead to poverty or pain, will not necessarily break off from it and reform. It is only when it is seen that sin is committed against God, and is evil in his sight, that it leads to a change of life.

Not to be repented of. Not to be regretted. It is permanent and abiding. There is no occasion to mourn over such repentance and change of life. It is that which the mind approves, and which it will always approve. There will be no reason for regretting it, and it will never be regretted. And it is so. Who ever yet repented of having truly repented of sin? Who is there, who has there ever been, who became a true penitent, and a true Christian, who ever regretted it? Not an individual has ever been known who regretted his having become a Christian. Not one who regretted that he had become one too soon in life, or that he had served the Lord Jesus too faithfully or too long.

But the sorrow of the world. All sorrow which is not toward God, and which does not arise from just views of sin as committed, against God, or lead to God. Probably Paul refers here to the sorrow which arises from worldly causes, and which does not lead to God for consolation. Such may be the sorrow which arises from the loss of friends or property; from disappointment, or, from shame and disgrace. Perhaps it may include the following things:

(1.) Sorrow arising from losses of property and friends, and from disappointment.

(2.) Sorrow for sin or vice when it overwhelms the mind with the consciousness of guilt, and when it does not lead to God, and when there is no contrition of soul from viewing it as an offence against God. Thus a female who has wandered from the paths of virtue, and involved her family and herself in disgrace; or a man who has been guilty of forgery, or perjury, or any other disgraceful crime, and who is detected; a man who has violated the laws of the land, and who has involved himself and family in disgrace, will often feel regret, and sorrow, and remorse, but it arises wholly from worldly considerations, and does not lead to God.

(3.) When the sorrow arises from a view of worldly consequences merely, and when there is no looking to God for pardon and consolation. Thus men, when they lose their property or friends, often pine in grief without looking to God. Thus when they have wandered from the path of virtue, and have fallen into sin, they often look merely to the disgrace among men, and see their names blasted, and their comforts gone, and pine away in grief. There is no looking to God for pardon or for consolation. The sorrow arises from this world, and it terminates there. It is the loss of what they valued pertaining to this world, and it is all which they had, and it produces death. It is sorrow such as the men of this World have--begins with this world, and terminates with this world.

<u>Worketh death.</u> Tends to death, spiritual, temporal, and eternal. It does not tend to life.

(1.) It produces distress only. It is attended with no consolation.

(2.) It tends to break the spirit, to destroy the peace, and to mar the happiness.

(3.) It often leads to death itself. The spirit is broken, and the heart pines away under the influence of the unalleviated sorrow; or under its influence men often lay violent hands on themselves, and take their lives. Life is often closed under the influence of such sorrow.

(4.) It tends to eternal death. There is no looking to God; no looking for pardon. It produces murmuring, repining, complaining, fretfulness against God, and thus leads to his displeasure, and to the condemnation and ruin of the soul.

{a} "sorrow worketh repentance" Jer 31:9; Eze 7:16

{b} "sorrow of the world" Pr 17:22

From William Burkitt's Expository Notes is the following.

"Note here, that sorrow for sin, will be of no advantage or avail upon us, if it be not godly sorrow, or a sorrow according to God, as it runs in the original.

Now it may be called a sorrow according to God, when it is a sorrow wrought in us by the Spirit of God, in obedience to the command of God, and with an eye at the glory of God; when it has sin, and not wrath, for its object; sin, as a wrong to God, as a contempt of his sovereignty, and a contrariety to his holiness.

Again, It is then a godly sorrow, when it puts us upon an high prizing of Jesus Christ, who became a sacrifice for sin; and prompts us to a cordial and unfeigned forsaking of all sin to such a turning from it, as is resolved against all returning to it.

The sorrow of the world may be taken two ways,

1. For the sorrow of worldly men, whose sorrow for sin is only a vexing of their hearts, not a breaking or humbling of their hearts; which being separate from true faith, and without any purpose to leave sin, worketh death, by wearing out the natural life lingeringly, and sometimes destroying the natural life violently, as in the case of Judas.

2. By the sorrow of the world, may be understood a sorrow for worldly things, a sorrow for worldly losses and disappointments. This is sinful, when it is excessive; and as it is prejudicial to the soul, so doth it hurt the body, and it hasteneth death. Worldly sorrow is a killing sorrow: Godly sorrow worketh repentance: But the sorrow of the world worketh death."

Then from the Family Bible Notes comes,

"Godly sorrow; such as God requires; which grieves for sin because it dishonors God.

Repentance to salvation; that sorrow for sin which leads a man to forsake it, and look to Christ for salvation. Not to be repented of; a change that will never be regretted or renounced. Sorrow of the world; that which is supremely selfish, and grieves principally because of the evil which sin occasions to the transgressor. Worketh death; tends to undermine health, shorten life, and hurry men to the second death."

From Spurgeon's Morning and Evening Devotions he wrote,

"Genuine, spiritual mourning for sin is the work of the Spirit of God. Repentance is too choose a flower to grow in nature's garden. Pearls grow naturally in oysters, but penitence never shows itself in sinners except divine grace works it in them. If thou hast one particle of real hatred for sin, God must have given it thee, for human nature's thorns never produced a single fig. "That which is born of the flesh is flesh."

True repentance has a distinct reference to the Saviour. <u>When we repent of sin, we must have one eye upon sin and another upon the cross, or it will be better still if we fix both our eyes upon Christ and see our transgressions only, in the light of His love.</u>

True sorrow for sin is eminently practical. No man may say he hates sin, if he lives in it.

Repentance makes us see the evil of sin, not merely as a theory, but experimentally--as a burnt child dreads fire. We shall be as much afraid of it, as a man who has lately been stopped and robbed is afraid of the thief upon the highway; and we shall shun it--shun it in everything--not in great things only, but in little things, as men shun little vipers as well as great snakes. True mourning for sin will make us very jealous over our tongue, lest it should say a wrong word; we shall be very watchful over our daily actions, lest in anything we offend, and each night we shall close the day with painful confessions of shortcoming, and each morning awaken with anxious prayers, that this day God would hold us up that we may not sin against Him.

Sincere repentance is continual. Believers repent until their dying day. This dropping well is not intermittent. Every other sorrow yields to time, but this dear sorrow grows with our growth, and it is so sweet a bitter, that we thank God we are permitted to enjoy and to suffer it until we enter our eternal rest."

Repentance always has to do with some level of sorrow or grief both before salvation and after. Even God felt some compunction, not of His sin, but of the sin of mankind in Genesis 6:5 & 6 which states,

"And GOD saw that the wickedness of man was great in the earth, and that every imagination of the thoughts of his heart was only evil continually. And it repented the LORD that he had made man on the earth, and it grieved him at his heart."

Notice the grief God felt over the wickedness of man. The author of the Family Bible Notes wrote on this,

"Repented the Lord—it grieved him; he would change his conduct towards men, as men change their conduct when sorry for what they have done; and instead of continuing them on the earth and granting them his favors, as he had done, he would destroy them."

The word repent comes from two Latin words which are "re" meaning "Back or again or to do again," and "pent" which comes from the Latin "Paena" meaning "pain." This is why I say, as do others as you have read that repentance always involves some level of pain or remorse. The words conviction and compunction are also always used in connection with repentance.

From Strong's Concordance the word repent means to think differently or afterwards, that is reconsider (morally to feel compunction.)

Thayer's says repent means to change one's mind; to change one's mind for better, heartily to amend with abhorrence of over past sins.

Repent in another source means the following,

1. To feel pain or regret for something done or spoken.
2. To express sorrow for something past

3. To change the mind in consequences of the inconvenience or injury done by past conduct.
4. In theology, to sorrow or be pained for sins. As a violation of God's Holy law, a dishonor to His character and government, and the foulest ingratitude to a Being of infinite benevolence.
5. To remember with sorrow, as to repent rash words; to repent an injury done to a neighbor, to repent of follies and vices.

Another source describes it thus, "In theology, the pain, regret or afflictions a person feels on account of his past conduct because it exposes him to punishment. This sorrow proceeding merely from the fear of punishment is called "legal repentance" as being excited by the terrors of legal penalties and it may exist without an amendment of life. Real penitence; sorrow or deep contrition for sin, as an offense and dishonor to God, a violation of His holy law, and the basest ingratitude towards Him. This is called "evangelical repentance" and is accompanied and followed by amendment of life."

Other statements say, "Repentance is a change of mind, or a conversion from sin to God." Yet another one says, "Repentance is the relinquishment of any practice, from conviction that it has offended God." Are you getting the idea from this that repentance involves a conviction and change of mind about sin?

John Gill wrote on Acts 26:20 about the phrase,

> "...that they should repent, "...that is they should repent of their sins; of sin in general, as it is committed against God, is a transgression of His law, and as it is in itself exceeding sinful, and in its effects dreadful." Later he wrote, "(this repentance) is an evangelical repentance; which has along with it faith in Christ."

On Matthew 3:8 which speaks of bringing forth fruits that are meet for repentance Gill wrote,

"...repentance is known by good works; these are fruits and effects of repentance, and which proof with men of sincerity of it." Repentance means a turning from sin.

Spurgeon in All of Grace said,

"To repent is to change your mind about sin, and Christ, and all the things of God. There is sorrow implied in this; but the main point is the turning of the heart from sin to Christ. It there is this turning, you have the essence of true repentance, even though no alarm and no despair should ever cast their shadow upon your mind."

In chapter 15 of the same book about Spurgeon are the following,

Page 170 – "It cannot be that pardon of sin should be given an impenitent sinner: this was to confirm him in his evil ways, and to teach him to think little of evil."

Page 171 – "I cannot tell what innumerable mischiefs would certainly occur if you could divide repentance and forgiveness, and pass by the sin while the sinner remained as fond of it as ever. In the very nature of things, if we believe in the holiness of God, it must be so, that if we continued in our sin, and will not repent of it, we cannot be forgiven, but must feel the consequence of our obstinacy. According to the infinite goodness of God, we are promised that if we will forsake our sins, confessing them, and will, by faith, accept the grace which is provided in Christ Jesus, God is faithful and just to forgive us our sins, and to cleanse us from all unrighteousness. (1 John 1:9). But, so long as God lives, there can be no promise of mercy to those who continue in their evil ways and refuse to acknowledge their wrongdoing."

Page 172 – "that mercy which could forgive the sin and yet let the sinner live in it would be scant and superficial mercy."

Page 173 – "But if we could be forgiven and then could be permitted to love sin, to riot in iniquity, and to wallow in lust, what would be the use of such forgiveness?"

Page 175 – "There never was a person yet who did unfeignedly repent of sin with believing repentance who was not forgiven; and on the other hand, there never was a person forgiven who had not repented of his sin. I do not hesitate to say that beneath the copes of heaven thee never was, there is not, and there never will be, any case of sin being washed away, unless at the same time the heart was led to repentance and faith in Christ. Hatred of sin and a sense of pardon come together into the soul, and abide together."

Hey, don't get upset with me I am just showing you Scripturally and historically what repent does and has meant.

From the King James Dictionary comes this…

Repent – To lament one's actions; turn again.

"True repentance is not just a changing of the mind, but a changing of the mind because of a sorrow or compunction (pricking of heart, poignant grief or remorse proceeding from consciousness of guilt; the pain of sorrow of regret for having offended God, and incurred His wrath) for something."

Sin and repentance have no compunction anymore because of our watered down teaching about them. The sting of sin is gone and the sting of repentance is also not there as it should be. Sin is no longer exceeding sinful, but culturally accepted. Repentance is just a by-word anymore meaning no more than going from unbelief to belief. The demons believe, yet they have more sense and compunction than most people, at least they tremble!

In Acts 17:3 it says that all men everywhere are to repent! Does that mean we are to go from unbelief to unbelief only? Yes! But the vehicle that gets us there is seeing our sinfulness, "For all have sinned and come short of the glory of God!" Again, when we are convicted of sin, we see our need of a Saviour and we turn to Him. Acts 20:21 states,

"Testifying both to the Jews, and also to the Greeks, repentance toward God, and faith toward our Lord Jesus Christ."

Adam Clarke commented on this saying,

"Repentance toward God, etc. - As all had sinned against God, so all should humble themselves before him against whom they have sinned; but humiliation is no atonement for sin; therefore repentance is insufficient, unless faith in our Lord Jesus Christ accompany it. Repentance disposes and prepares the soul for pardoning mercy; but can never be considered as making compensation for past acts of transgression. This repentance and faith were necessary to the salvation both of Jews and Gentiles; for all had sinned, and come short of God's glory. The Jews must repent, who had sinned so much, and so long, against light and knowledge. The Gentiles must repent, whose scandalous lives were a reproach to man. Faith in Jesus Christ was also indispensably necessary; for a Jew might repent, be sorry for his sin, and suppose that, by a proper discharge of his religious duty, and bringing proper sacrifices, he could conciliate the favor of God: No, this will not do; nothing but faith in Jesus Christ, as the end of the law, and the great and only vicarious sacrifice, will do; hence he testified to them the necessity of faith in this Messiah. The Gentiles might repent of their profligate lives, turn to the true God, and renounce all idolatry: this is well, but it is not sufficient: they also have sinned, and their present amendment and faith can make no atonement for what is past; therefore, they also must believe on the Lord Jesus, who died for their sins, and rose again for their justification."

Albert Barnes wrote,

"Repentance toward God. Repentance is to be exercised "toward God," because...

(1.) sin has been committed against him, and it is proper that we express our sorrow to the Being whom we have offended; and,

(2.) because God only can pardon. Sincere repentance exists only where there is a willingness to make acknowledgment to the very being whom we have offended or injured.

And faith toward. In regard to; in; confidence in the work and merits of the Lord Jesus. This is required, because there is no other one who can save from sin."

John Gill puts it this way,

"Testifying both to the Jews, and also to the Greeks,.... To the Jews first in their synagogue, and then to both Jews and Greeks, or Gentiles, in the school of Tyrannus; opening and explaining to both the nature and use, urging and insisting upon, and proving by undeniable testimonies the necessity,

of repentance toward God and faith toward our Lord Jesus Christ: the former of these is not a legal repentance, but an evangelical one; which flows from a sense of the love of God, and an application of pardoning grace and mercy, and is always attended with hope, at least of interest in it, and as here with faith in Christ Jesus: it lies in a true sight and sense of sin, as exceeding sinful, being contrary to the nature and law of God, and a deformation of the image of God in man, as well as followed with dreadful and pernicious consequences; and in a godly sorrow for it, as it is committed against a God of infinite purity and holiness, and of love, grace, and mercy; and it shows itself in shame for sin, and blushing at it, and in an ingenious confession of it, and forsaking it: and the latter of these is not an historical faith, or an assent of the mind to whatsoever is true concerning the person, office, and grace of Christ; but is a spiritual act of the soul upon him; it is a looking and going out to him, a laying hold and leaning on him, and trusting in him, for grace, righteousness, peace, pardon, life, and salvation. Now these two were the sum of the apostle's ministry; this is a breviary or compendium of it; a form of sound words held fast and published by him: and as these two go together as doctrines in the ministry of the word, they go together as graces in the experience of the saints; where the one is, there the other is; they are wrought in the soul at one and the same time, by one and the same hand; the one is not before the other in order of time, however it may be in order of working, or as to visible observation; repentance is mentioned before faith, not that it precedes it, though it may be discerned in its outward acts before it; yet faith as to its inward exercise on Christ is full as early, if not earlier; souls first look to Christ by faith, and then they mourn in tears of evangelical repentance, Zec_12:10 though the order of the Gospel ministry is very fitly here expressed, which is first to lay before sinners the evil of sin, and their danger by it, in order to convince of it, and bring to repentance for it; and then to direct and encourage them to faith in Christ Jesus, as in the case of the jailer, Act_16:29 and this is, generally speaking, the order and method in which the Holy Spirit proceeds; he is first a spirit of conviction and illumination, he shows to souls the exceeding sinfulness of sin, causes them to loath it and themselves for it, and humbles them under a sense of it; and then he is a spirit of faith, he reveals Christ unto them as God's way or salvation, and works faith in them to believe in him. Moreover, these two, repentance and faith, were the two parts of Christ's ministry, Mar_1:15 and are what, he would have published and insisted on, in the preaching of the word, Luk_24:47 so that the ministry of the apostle was very conformable to the mind and will of Christ."

In 2 Kings Chapter 22, King Josiah was having the temple restored. In verse 8 it says,

"And Hilkiah the high priest said unto Shaphan the scribe, I have found the book of the law in the house of the LORD. And Hilkiah gave the book to Shaphan, and he read it."

They had found it (the Scriptures) meaning they did not know before where it was. Since they did not know where the

Scripture were, they had not read it for a while. But, oh, when they did, look at what happened in verses 9 through 11...

"And Shaphan the scribe came to the king, and brought the king word again, and said, Thy servants have gathered the money that was found in the house, and have delivered it into the hand of them that do the work, that have the oversight of the house of the LORD. And Shaphan the scribe shewed the king, saying, Hilkiah the priest hath delivered me a book. And Shaphan read it before the king. And it came to pass, when the king had heard the words of the book of the law, that he rent his clothes."

The reading of the Word of God brought CONVICTION OF SIN! What do you do with conviction of sin? To the people of Israel God was not happy, but to the king is this promise...

2 Kings 22:19 & 20

" Because thine heart was tender, and thou hast humbled thyself before the LORD, when thou heardest what I spake against this place, and against the inhabitants thereof, that they should become a desolation and a curse, and hast rent thy clothes, and wept before me; I also have heard thee, saith the LORD. Behold therefore, I will gather thee unto thy fathers, and thou shalt be gathered into thy grave in peace; and thine eyes shall not see all the evil which I will bring upon this place. And they brought the king word again."

But the king being a good and godly leader was not happy with that. He was concerned for his nation and took steps to rectify the problem. The verses in chapter 22 that tell of the displeasure of God on the people says,

2 Kings 22:16 & 17

"Thus saith the LORD, Behold, I will bring evil upon this place, and upon the inhabitants thereof, even all the words of the book which the king of Judah hath read: Because they have forsaken me,

and have burned incense unto other gods, that they might provoke me to anger with all the works of their hands; therefore my wrath shall be kindled against this place, and shall not be quenched."

After was a great revival where the king and all the people got rid of the idols, they turned from their wicked ways and got God's attention!

When Nathan the prophet went before King David and rebuked him for the sin he had committed with Bathsheba and all that was connected with it, conviction of sin gripped David who then cried out, "I have sinned against the Lord…" (2 Samuel 12:13) From this we have Psalm 51:1-19 which is the prayer of David dealing with this event. Look at it now…

"To the chief Musician, A Psalm of David, when Nathan the prophet came unto him, after he had gone in to Bathsheba. Have mercy upon me, O God, according to thy lovingkindness: according unto the multitude of thy tender mercies blot out my transgressions. Wash me throughly from mine iniquity, and cleanse me from my sin. For I acknowledge my transgressions: and my sin is ever before me. Against thee, thee only, have I sinned, and done this evil in thy sight: that thou mightest be justified when thou speakest, and be clear when thou judgest. Behold, I was shapen in iniquity; and in sin did my mother conceive me. Behold, thou desirest truth in the inward parts: and in the hidden part thou shalt make me to know wisdom. Purge me with hyssop, and I shall be clean: wash me, and I shall be whiter than snow. Make me to hear joy and gladness; that the bones which thou hast broken may rejoice. Hide thy face from my sins, and blot out all mine iniquities. Create in me a clean heart, O God; and renew a right spirit within me. Cast me not away from thy presence; and take not thy holy spirit from me. Restore unto me the joy of thy salvation; and uphold me with thy free spirit. Then will I teach transgressors thy ways; and sinners shall

be converted unto thee. Deliver me from bloodguiltiness, O God, thou God of my salvation: and my tongue shall sing aloud of thy righteousness. O Lord, open thou my lips; and my mouth shall shew forth thy praise. For thou desirest not sacrifice; else would I give it: thou delightest not in burnt offering. The sacrifices of God are a broken spirit: a broken and a contrite heart, O God, thou wilt not despise. Do good in thy good pleasure unto Zion: build thou the walls of Jerusalem. Then shalt thou be pleased with the sacrifices of righteousness, with burnt offering and whole burnt offering: then shall they offer bullocks upon thine altar."

Does that sound like someone who flippantly takes for granted what he had done? Or was there some contrition, some broken heartedness? Yes, there was some real repentance going on here with the conviction of the Holy Spirit in action in his life.

David was not getting saved here; this is repentance after he had been saved. Repentance of sin begins at salvation and continues as we grow in Christ. My whole point in this is NOT to say that we must repent of sin only at salvation, repentance of sin, again, also takes place after salvation as we learn about sin in Scriptures, through preaching and yielding to His leading.

Who among us is the same after we trusted Christ? Was there not a difference in our lives after we trusted Christ for our salvation? Were there not things we did before salvation that we changed immediately after salvation? Were we the same after salvation as we were before salvation? Not me! I immediately stopped some things in my life and I immediately started some things in my life the day of my salvation. Were you rebellious before salvation and more obedient after? All this is a result of seeing your sins and sinfulness and repenting of it. We then began growing as Christians as we read the Bible, listened to preaching, yielding to the Holy Spirit and watching and talking with other Christians. Were we perfect? No! But the path we were on started when we saw ourselves to some degree as God did. As we were drawing close to a Holy God, we saw our sins and sinfulness and had a change of mind about it.

Sin is exceeding sinful! If our righteousness's look likes filthy rags to a Holy God, WHAT MUST OUR SIN LOOK LIKE? We must put the sting, the pain of sin back into sin and quit making excuses for it. We need to once again thunder from the pulpits to REPENT!

CHAPTER TWELVE

Look for the Exit Sign!

1 Corinthians 10:13

"There hath no temptation taken you but such as is common to man: but God is faithful, who will not suffer you to be tempted above that ye are able; but will with the temptation also make a way to escape, that ye may be able to bear it."

In a previous chapter I showed you how many times we try to blame God for our sins saying, "He was testing me." Again, in James 1:13 it CLEARLY says,

"Let no man say when he is tempted, I am tempted of God: for God cannot be tempted with evil, neither tempteth he any man:"

So, how is it that we are so easily conquered by that sin which so easily besets us? The answer is that we sin because we want to. (James 1:14) We do not have to sin, but we do because we want to. We were born in iniquity according to Psalm 51:5 and that means that sin is as natural to us as walking and talking. Our parents did not have to teach us how to disobey, it came natural, and it was automatic and easy. But, as Christians we should eschew evil, should we sin? God forbids it! (Romans 6:1 & 2)

But, then again, we see the wail of Paul in Romans 7:15 when he said,

"For that which I do I allow not: for what I would, that do I not; but what I hate, that do I."

So, how can I stay away from sin, how can I stop? My answer and God's answer is, LOOK FOR THE EXIT SIGN!

If you have ever flown then you know the routine of the stewardesses who demonstrate how to buckle your seat belt. They then instruct you on how to put the oxygen mask on in case the cabin has lost is air pressure and tell you to breathe normally. I always laugh when they say that because if the cabin has lost its air pressure there is a BAD problem and everyone will be hyper-ventilating and screaming. I doubt anyone will be able to breathe normally. But they then tell you where the emergency exits are on the plane in case you need to get off quickly.

We also know that in any public building there are lighted exit signs above the doors to show you where to exit the building in case of an emergency. All of this is there to help us in an emergency where our lives could be in great jeopardy.

Well, God also has as exit sign for sin to help us escape its power over us. It is found in 1 Corinthians 10:13 which states,

> *"There hath no temptation taken you but such as is common to man: but God is faithful, who will not suffer you to be tempted above that ye are able; but will with the temptation also make a way to escape, that ye may be able to bear it."*

This is a long verse but it is one every Christian should memorize and study carefully.

We know that when we are tempted, according to James 1:14 that, "...everyman is tempted, when he is drawn away of his own lust and enticed." The reason we are tempted is because of our own lusts, or, we want to sin! When we want to sin, we should be looking for the exit sign, we should be looking for a way not to sin because there is always a way out, there is a way to escape!

Galatians 5:16 shows us one of the escape routes from temptation and sin.

> *"This I say then, Walk in the Spirit, and ye shall not fulfil the lust of the flesh."*

Remember what Paul said in Romans 7:18-25 which is included here.

Romans 7:18-25

"For I know that in me (that is, in my flesh,) dwelleth no good thing: for to will is present with me; but how to perform that which is good I find not. For the good that I would I do not: but the evil which I would not, that I do. Now if I do that I would not, it is no more I that do it, but sin that dwelleth in me. I find then a law, that, when I would do good, evil is present with me. For I delight in the law of God after the inward man: But I see another law in my members, warring against the law of my mind, and bringing me into captivity to the law of sin which is in my members. O wretched man that I am! who shall deliver me from the body of this death? I thank God through Jesus Christ our Lord. So then with the mind I myself serve the law of God; but with the flesh the law of sin."

There is that struggle which we all have until this mortal shall put on immortality and the corruptible puts on incorruption! Yet, we also understand that we will all be tempted and that our fleshly part of us will always struggle against the Spirit. But, we have an escape or a way out and that is to walk in the Spirit and ye SHALL NOT, SHALL NOT, **SHALL NOT** fulfill the lusts of the flesh! (Galatians 5:16) We are to also be, "…led of the Spirit…" (Galatians 5:18) Ok, then how do I do that?

Galatians 5 verses 19 and 22 tell us what to look for. If we are following the things of the flesh the fruit we will bear will be fleshly. On the other hand, if we are walking in the Spirit our fruit will be totally different from the fruit of the flesh. Let's look at these verses.

Galatians 5:16-26

"This I say then, Walk in the Spirit, and ye shall not fulfil the lust of the flesh. For the flesh lusteth against the Spirit, and the Spirit against the flesh: and these are contrary the one to the other: so that ye cannot do the things that ye would. But if ye be led of the Spirit, ye are not under the law.

Now the works of the flesh are manifest, which are these; Adultery, fornication, uncleanness, lasciviousness, Idolatry, witchcraft, hatred, variance, emulations, wrath, strife, seditions, heresies, Envyings, murders, drunkenness, revellings, and such like: of the which I tell you before, as I have also told you in time past, that they which do such things shall not inherit the kingdom of God. But the fruit of the Spirit is love, joy, peace, longsuffering, gentleness, goodness, faith, Meekness, temperance: against such there is no law. And they that are Christ's have crucified the flesh with the affections and lusts. If we live in the Spirit, let us also walk in the Spirit. Let us not be desirous of vain glory, provoking one another, envying one another."

You and I know when we are sinning! God also knows and He knows that He has made a way to escape…all we have to do is look for the exit sign and we should do it BEFORE WE TAKE THE NEXT STEP HEADED DOWN TO THE SIN AND GODS DISPLEASURE. He is faithful to make sure that we are not tempted above that which we are able to handle! He is faithful to make a way to escape. We just need to be faithful at doing what we know we are to do and to look for the escape from the temptation.

Sometimes the escape is just to look the other way or to stay away from certain places and people. Sometimes it is simple, other times more complex but one thing is for sure…there is a way to escape!

Jesus set a great example of how to handle temptation when He was tempted of the Devil after Jesus had fasted 40 days and nights. He quoted Scripture dealing with the temptation He was faced with. This means that we too should know the Scriptures well enough so that when we are tempted, we too can eliminate the temptation and not sin!

But, now I need to ask the question, what do we do when we do sin? Most of us know the verse below.

Proverbs 28:13

"He that covereth his sins shall not prosper: but whoso confesseth and forsaketh them shall have mercy."

Dear Christian friend, let's make sin exceeding sinful again! Let's always be on our guard understanding the Devil is a roaring lion seeking whom he may devour. Let's look at sin the way God does again because, if our righteousness's look like filthy rags to our God, what must our sins look like!

INDEX OF WORDS AND PHRASES

SCRIPTURE REFERENCES

Genesis 6:5
Genesis 6:6
Exodus 20:3-6
Exodus 20:14
Exodus 32:1
Exodus 32:7, 8
Leviticus 18:22
Numbers 14:26-37
Numbers 32:23
Deuteronomy 11:26-28
Deuteronomy 25:16
Judges 2:15
Judges 3:11, 12
Judges 4:1-24
Judges 6:1
Judges 8:32, 33
Judges 12:15
Judges 13:1
2 Samuel 11:27
2 Kings 22:8
2 Kings 22:9-11
2 Kings 22:16, 17
2 Kings 22:19, 20
1 Chronicles 10:13, 14
2 Chronicles 7:14
Job 7:17
Job 15:14
Job 15:20
Job 15:31
Psalms 5:4
Psalm 8:4
Psalm 11:5
Psalm 34:21
Psalm 37:28
Psalm 38:4
Psalm 38:5
Psalm 51:1-19

Psalm 51:3
Psalm 51:5
Psalm 51:9-15
Psalm 66:18
Psalm 107:17
Psalm 139:23, 24
Psalm 144:3
Proverbs 6:16-19
Proverbs 6:26
Proverbs 6:26-35
Proverbs 6:33
Proverbs 11:19
Proverbs 13:15
Proverbs 23:29-35
Proverbs 28:13
Ecclesiastes 2:26
Ecclesiastes 8:11-13
Isaiah 1:4
Isaiah 5:20
Isaiah 53:4-6
Isaiah 64:6
Jeremiah 3:12-15
Jeremiah 44:4
Jonah 3:4
Jonah 3:5-10
Zechariah 8:17
Matthew 3:8
Matthew 4:1-11
Matthew 5:16
Matthew 7:17-19
Matthew 12:35-37
Matthew 19:3-9
Matthew 28:20
Luke 5:1-7
Luke 11:4
Luke 16:15
John 8:31-34

Acts 17:3
Acts 20:21
Act 26:20
Romans 1:18-32
Romans 1:32
Romans 2:9
Romans 3:10
Romans 3 :12-18
Romans 3:20
Romans 3:23
Romans 5:6, 7
Romans 5:12
Romans 5:19
Romans 6:1-23
Romans 6:1, 2
Romans 6:13
Romans 6:15
Romans 6:16
Romans 6:19
Romans 6:21
Romans 6:23
Romans 7:5
Romans 7:13
Romans 7:7-13
Romans 7:15
Romans 7:14-25
Romans 8:6, 7
Romans 8:12, 13
Romans 12:1, 2
1 Corinthians 8:3
I Corinthians 10:13
2 Corinthians 5:10
2 Corinthians 5:21
2 Corinthians 7:10

Galatians 2:16
Galatians 2:21
Galatians 3:10
Galatians 3:24
Galatians 5:16-18
Galatians 5:19-26
Galatians 6:7-8
Ephesians 2:8-10
Colossians 1:9, 10
1 Timothy 1:8-11
1 Timothy 1:12-16
1 Timothy 4:8
Titus 3:14
Hebrews 1:8
Hebrews 1:9
Hebrews 4:15
Hebrews 7:26, 27
Hebrews 12:2
Hebrews 12:5-7
Hebrews 13:5
James 1:12-25
James 2:8-11
1 Peter 2:6-10
1 Peter 2:21-24
1 Peter 5:8, 9
2 Peter 2:8
2 Peter 2:12-19
2 Peter 3:9
1 John 2:3
1 John 3:1-3
1 John 3:4
1 John 5:3
Revelation 13:17, 18

ABOUT THE AUTHOR

I was born in 1950 and born again in 1973. I began preaching and being a personal soul winner in 1975 not knowing what the Lord had for me to do but now after 40 plus years of preaching and winning people to Christ I have been used both nationally and in some foreign countries. All the glory goes to our Lord and Saviour Jesus Christ in it all. I have been used to start a church in Delaware, Ohio from 1982 until 1995. In 1995 I resigned as Pastor and started my work as an Evangelist.

My wife and I were married in 1973 and now have 3 daughters who are all serving the Lord with their husbands and families in different parts of America. They have blessed us with 11 grandchildren many of whom have been saved.

I have my Bachelor's degree in Pastoral Theology from Hyles Anderson College (1982); my Master's degree in Ministry from Bethany Theological Seminary and an honorary Doctor of Divinity from what was Texas Baptist College but now called Texas Independent Baptist Seminary and Schools.

.

www.ingramcontent.com/pod-product-compliance
Lightning Source LLC
LaVergne TN
LVHW051128080426
835510LV00018B/2289